AF229150

A CULINARY OF POEMS

TOPCAT

Having grown up in the suburbs of Western Sydney and developing a fondness for all that is Australian, It has been a dream to share my thoughts in poetry about some of the iconic elements and memories I have treasured from childhood.

The opportunity came in the form of care, love and encouragement from close friends such as Michelle G (editing), Wes P (advice), Karyn S (advice) and Steph H (editing) together with the skills of Stephanie Poleson who created some amazing illustrations and the book creating knowledge of my good friend Simon Creedy for his ability to guide me in the final formatting and publishing of my book *A Culinary of Poems.*

Tonie Christian (TOPCAT) - Author

Illustrations by **Stephanie Poleson**
Book Layout by **Simon Creedy**

© 2024 COPYRIGHT BLACK CAT PUBLISHING

IN LOVING MEMORY

In memory of my late sister Dana Maree Therese.
And my late Grandmothers Louisa Ya-Pidik
and Jean Nellie.

BEAUTIFUL

Beautiful begins from love within.

It's nurtured from the heart

And in the soul where we begin.

We come in to the universe

By land and sea.

A testament of life be our destiny.

CONTENTS

The Aussie Magpie · 1

Ode to The Blues · 3

Me Lil' Nation - Canberra · 5

Ode to The Busby Warriors (Old Spirits Never Die) · 7

My Semillon Sauvignon · 9

The Light Horsemen (The ANZACS) · 11

Bells Line Road · 13

Ode to Shane Keith Warne · 15

Ode to Animal Spirits of Ash & Dust (Bushfire 2019/20) · 17

A Billy and Tetley Blue · 19

Rickety Rattler Ghost Carriages (Red Rattlers) · 21

The Blue Mountains (The Beast Within) · 23

Bottle Brush Tree · 25

The '1982 Kangaroos' (The Invincible's) · 27

The Legend Fisher's Ghost · 29

Tasmania (The Last Great Wilderness) · 31

Jimi Hendrix (Club 27) · 33

Bushranger (The Gallop) · 35

Eucalyptus Tree (Old Gum Tree) · 37

Connoisseur · 39

Wayne 'Jnr' Pearce							41

State of Origin (NRL)							43

Halloween (Frightfully Scary)						45

Shaman									47

Leopard									49

Penny 'The Beatles' Lane						51

How to Make A Winter's Flu						53

Henry 'Jack' Avery (King of Pirates)					55

Queen of Hearts							57

Frogs and Toads							59

A Wish									61

Santa's Sleigh								63

The Lil' Aussie Ocker							65

Road to The Golden Guitar (Tamworth)					67

Chocolat								69

Gothic									71

My Sunburnt Country (Australia)					73

The Goldy Mermaid							75

The Currawong (Dark Shadows)						77

Autumn in Orange (NSW)						79

THE AUSSIE MAGPIE

That little magpie
Is Aussie as can be.
He's more indigenous
Than you and me.
With his distinctive voice
And steely eyed stare.
He'll hoodwink you blindly
With his jovial glare.

His sharp pointed beak
Loves to peck and reek
Likes to manicure lawns
As he forages for the meek.

His black and white colour
His distinguished tux
He goes about his business
Securing his tuft.

Up at the break of dawn
When your snuggled in your bubble
He'll be up singing and calling
In his muddle.
Especially at that time of the year
When he leaves you
Fending in a huddle of fear.

As a little lone preacher
Glaring at the sun
Or times working
With the farmers
Digging up for fun.

On cold winter mornings
And pipping hot days.
He scrounges and digs
And sticks his beak into clay.

On green grassy flats
He scurries on the ground.
Catching gizzards
And always looking down.
And bops his head
Like a little circus clown.
As he lives in every big city
And in every little town.

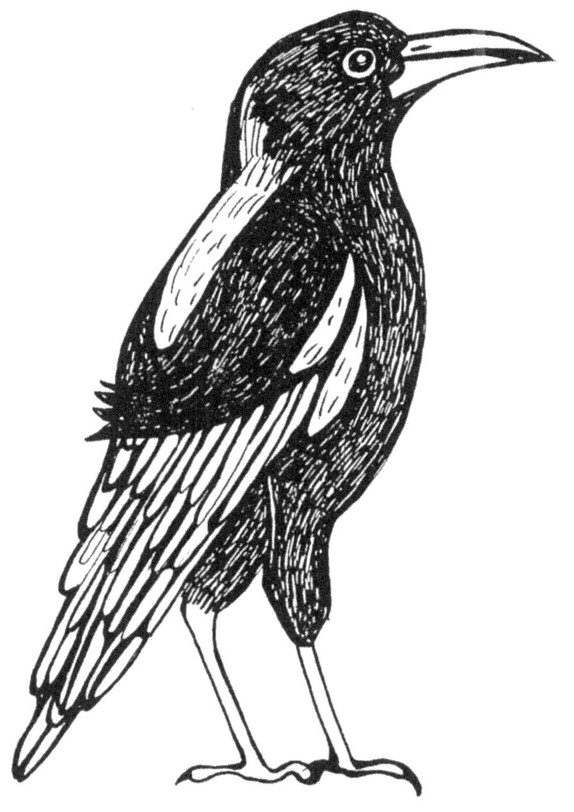

ODE TO THE BLUES

South of the border
South to the Mississippi
Where the 'Blues' where born
In a land of opportunity.

On the bayou
And the everglades.
Where the voices of ghosts
Of slaves.
Sang songs and worked
The cotton fields
And sugar mills.

Voodoo dolls
And witchcraft
And magic potions.
And snake charms.

A chant from the rhythm
And songs from the soul.
Where you come to the crossroads
Where the devil played the blues
To Robert Johnson's soul.

A lady sings the blues
Was Billie Holiday.
And Ella Fitzgeralds
Pizazz was jazz.

As cool as Muddy Waters
To BB Kings guitar,
And John Lee Hookers boogie woo-gee
On his electric guitar.

As rock and roll was to Elvis,
As the Rolling Stones
Was rhythm guitar.

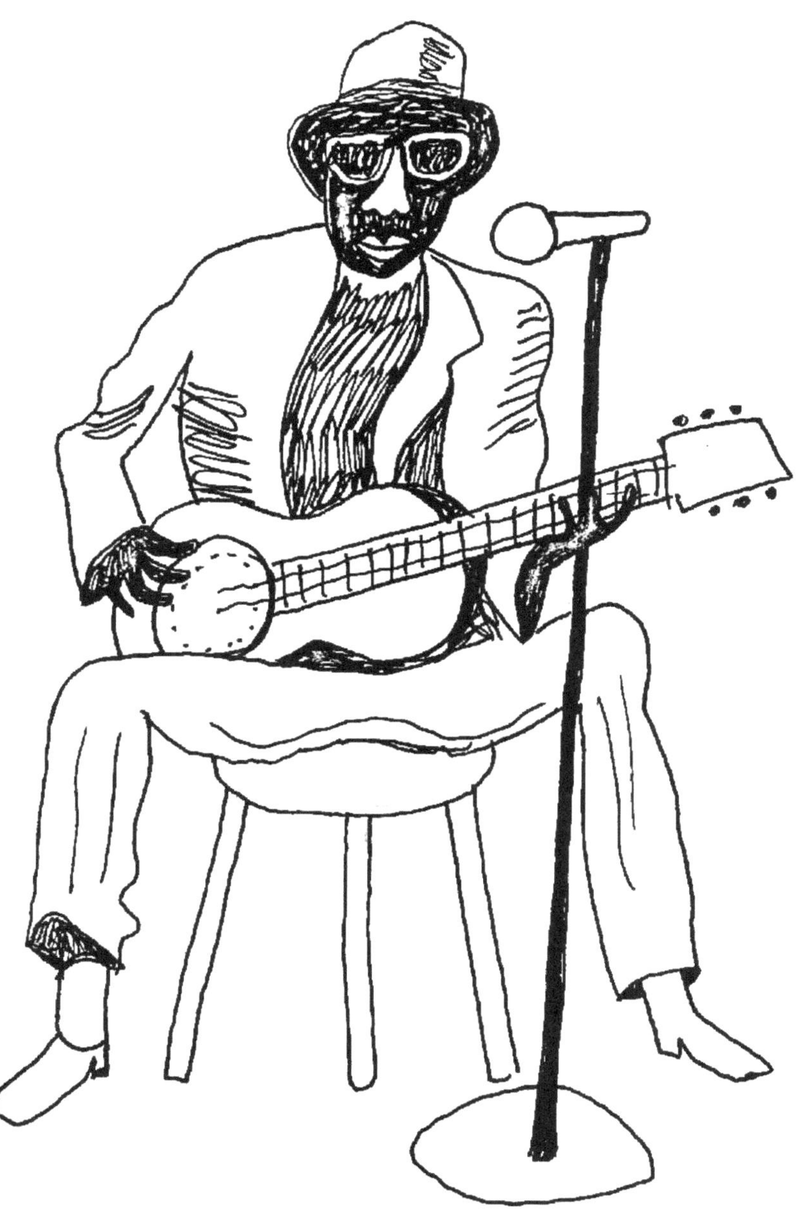

ME LIL' NATION - CANBERRA

I drive into Canberra
On Northbourne I pass.
Yowanii to the right
With its green blade of grass.
Maybe have a swing
Or birdie or par.
Or order a bitters
With me name at the bar.

On ward I drive
To shops nearby.
Where a beggar rustles
For dollars and fives.
Further I drive
To me nest on the left.
It feels like a forrest
But to me it's me rest.

The trams are new
As red and fast.
They run up and down
One needs to be nimble
One needs to be fast.

I wonder down to Capital Hill
Just after Floriade I hit the till.
And watch those pollies
Twitch'n their thumbs
As they whine about the economy
Watchin my lovely dollar
Fall into buggery.

I'll have a swig and a jig in town
Tonite at O' Malley's bright lights
I'll wear his crown,
Or watch me Brumbies
Run loose on the field

And those mIghty Raiders looking
For another title to fill.

I'll drive to Manuka just for a look
Or test tasting my taste bud
... Especially the reds.
I'll breathe in that crisp
Cold Canberra air.
With a touch of gumtree
That purifies my lair.

Yet there's nothing
Like Canberra that amazes.
In its Spring of gumtree
And Wattle of oasis.

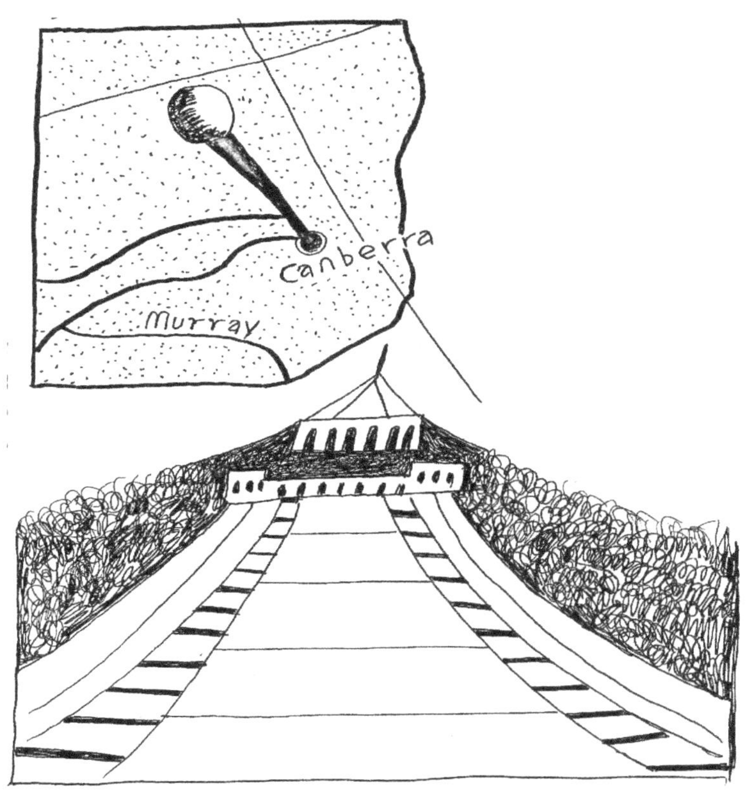

ODE TO THE BUSBY WARRIORS (OLD SPIRITS NEVER DIE)

Busby Warriors.
Busby pride.
The once little club
For the little guy.
The jerseys of old
Weren't so fancy
But what it made up for
Was all heart and glory.

Maroon and blue
You stood ten feet tall
With toughness even
If you were small.
A suburban town
A few people around.
A dog and a case of beer.
God touched an era
From all grades to
The under 7's that year.

You trained the week
The coaches speech.
Then the captain
Does all the talking.
On the Saturday
The young warriors play
With their heart on their sleeve
And rugby league.

Local fans together for a chat
Laughs and a can of beer
Meat pie, sausage roll
Mum and dads and kids trade hellos'
You played rough you played tough.

One for all and all for one
It was all blood, sweat and tears.
We had all those moves
Those fancy grooves
Even for the girls.

You tackled hard you did the yards
From the backs to the forwards.
Old Red on empty legs
Courageous Cass and tough old Stark.
To Snapper (the number 7), Micky Lenf …
And Mr Ward … to Mr Farmers barging runs.
Charismatic Lazz and tuff Selb and Rob
And to a young Mel on debut.

We did it all in '83'
To win at Ringrose Park
To win the premiership for the glory
By gees that's all we asked.

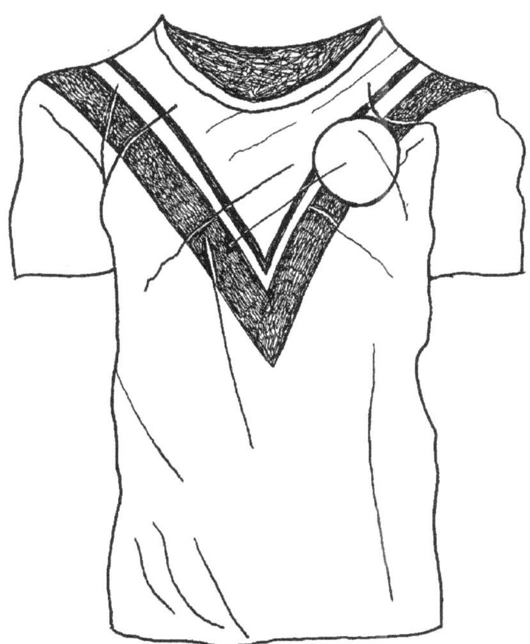

MY SEMILLON SAUVIGNON

Not to dry
Not too bland.
Nice and chilled it's that
Glass in my hand.

On a hot summers day
In that midday sun.
Beats down on me
Like a loaded gun.

With a breath off fresh air
In that searing heat.
When you can only hear cicadas
Sing in their musical beat.

And the sweat on my brow
As it runs down my neck
I can look forward to
Quenching my thirst.

With the grapes of wrath
That's one mighty thirst.
From its great harvest
I quench my first
(If its the last drink
On this earth).

I look at that bottle
It's crystal clear
To saviour a moment
Before it disappears.

And the whiff and
The aroma of alcohol
And a hint of tropical
That saviours my soul.

Down she goes filling my drought
Touching and awakening my every side.
As a drought of relief till it satisfies
My inner appetite.

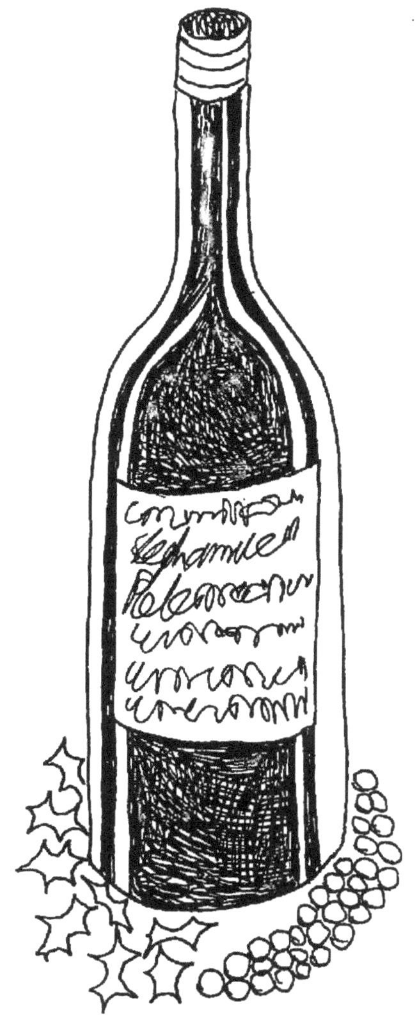

THE LIGHT HORSEMEN
(THE ANZACS)

The light horsemen
Upon they ride.
They rise into the thousands
Into what abides.

A tackle en-misson
On the lonely plight
As a grant for the sovereign and crown
As we children go to fight.

Merciless and harrow west point blank.
Dust and garrisons
And an army of legends
And folklore gents.

Their steads back cracked by the whip
Of the muster and shellac from the arid landeric.
This Brumby the strong of spirit within
They run the narrow with the weight
They carry heavy but thin.
A cavalcade thickened and downed
From the cold mountains
(With nostrils of fire from the devils own furnace).

The soldier of stockman suitor
Is mooted for a young gentlemen
With bloodline astuitor.
From the belly of Irish and English
And what they can muster
Be non-English and the indigenous.

As they ride into the dawn
With the stench of gunpowder drawn.
The dust and dry of a desert lawn
For here lies Beersheba.

The whole fifteen thousand
There's no time for fuss.
But for courage and crown
In fear but trust.
The charge of the light brigade
Seize the dawn.
As the Anzac troops
And alliance claim victory
On them's green lawn.

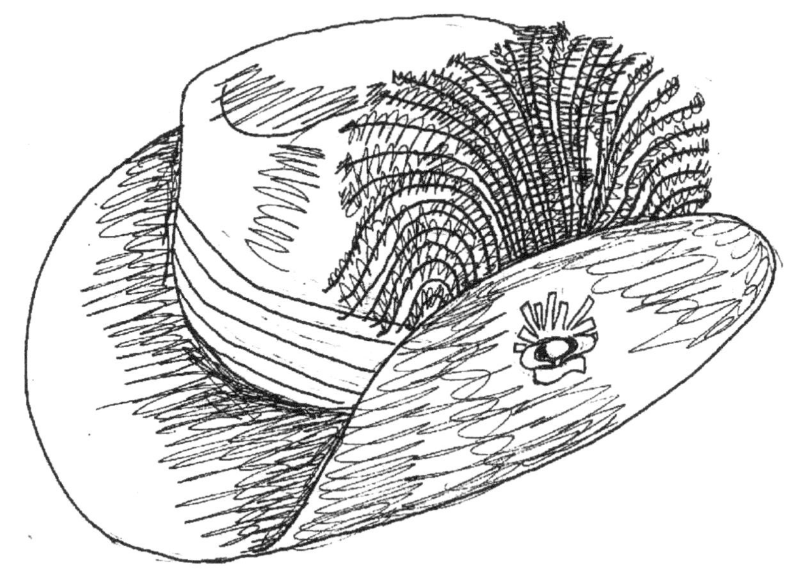

BELLS LINE ROAD

The Bells Line Road
Before you follow.
Before the dark
And winding, windy narrow.

As it straightens and veers
Unwinding turn ...
You grip the bend
As you come down to third.
You top up the gear
To climb the first.
There's more commotion
To swallow your thirst.

A chance, a scent
To bury some dust.
To cleanse some habit
Leaving drivers eating their dust.
But no time to rebel
In your mind you trust.

Don't leave you hand
Your faith with swallow
Hands on the steering wheel
More road than tallow.
A heavenly sent of green house musk
That cleanses your pallet
Like wine and husk.

Bridges ascend to an open sky
Recommend and follow
And climb up high (like a bird in the sky).
Then descend and mend ...
And settle as a cusp of dusk
As the evening falls it reeks
Of natures musk.

Through summer and rain, dry and sleet
It steals the earth on your rubber feet.
Through sludge and ice
And shadows of fright.
As light begins to shine
At the end of your plight.

Your mind will ease and time to wallow
As you drive through flats and fairy meadow.
One presses on much haste but mellow
To immerse with precision
Towards the town you follow.

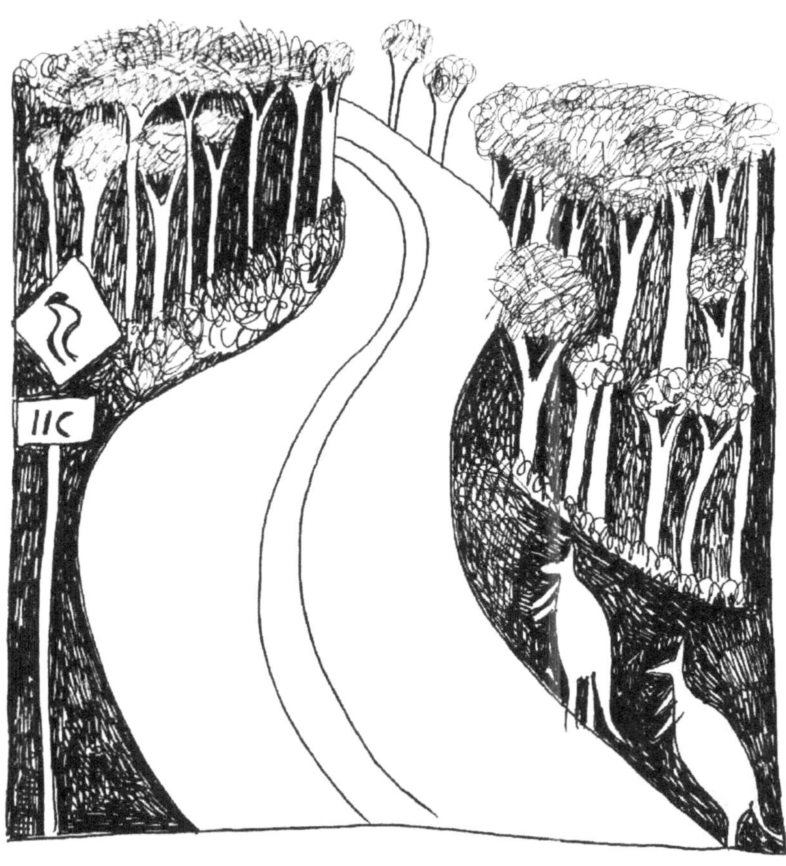

ODE TO SHANE KEITH WARNE

As the MCG hill erupts.
And echoes of Warr–nee
A sombre moment
For his last over and glory.
Now he rests
With the greats of the game.
If not too early will pave his name.

So he liked to smoke.
So he liked to party
And liked loud music
The drink and the ladies.
(That's just the boy
who grew up in the '80s)

The lovable larrikin
And times joking fanatican.
The greatest leg spinner
To grace the game
To wear the 'baggy green'
In its cotton and fame.

A Victorian and bloody marvellous
By his contemporaries.
As Bill and Ritchie loved him
With his rockstar fame.
He was brash, he was sass.
He was the X factor
He was the Mr Razzmatazz
He brought Test Match cricket
Back from the brink
Into rockstar pizzazz.

He could bowel 'em
Not throw 'em.
He knew how to dish 'em up
And deliver 'em.
The wrung-un, the googley
And his famous flipper
He bamboozled them all-
(Even 'Gatting' the nonchalance)

He bagged them here
he bagged them there.
All seven hundred and eight scalps.
From every bloody where.
And his lesser crime his ODI

He had his critics
Ohhh cowardly antics.
And even the Queen
Was in awe of his cheeks antics.
But he will always be young
And forever stay young
Our own Shane Warrrnee.

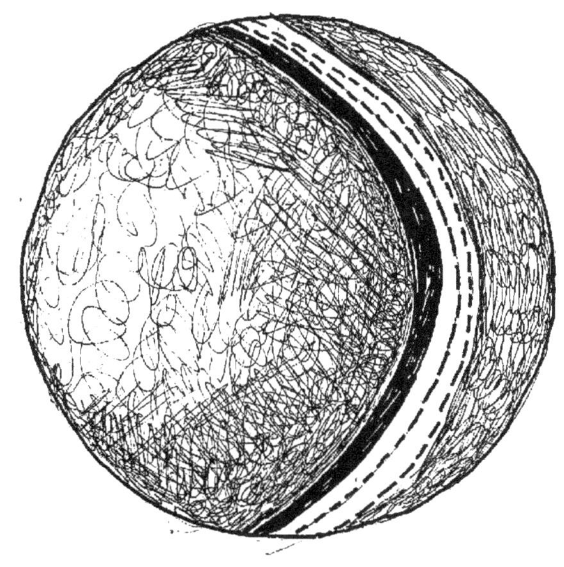

ODE TO ANIMAL SPIRITS OF ASH & DUST (BUSHFIRE 2019/20)

Shadow upon shadow
Came to claim great numbers.
Through day and night
There was no slumber.
The fires came angry
And in numbers from hell
On wheels and army of devils as well.

With no respite
God but tried to fight
God tried to help the little souls
But too many claws and paws
And web feet to hold.

No pitter patter
Or ruffle of feathers
Nor sleepy breeze
Or splashing through water.
No rummaging through woods
Or burrowing through girth
Or squeaky see-saw
Or slithering through earth.

Our animal friends
Never stood a chance.
No cry for help
Nor shoulder to defend.
No footprints left
Or trails unturned
Just gone in seconds
Not a voice to yearn.

Somehow humans
Tried to intervene
To no prevail
But sorry and mean.
Just leave their little souls
Lay bare for the breeze.
To toil over their bones
To ashes then dust to add ease.

Silence in lakes
And streams you swam.
And billabongs you shared
Is spared no friends.
No footprints left
Or bird of a nest.
And trails and burrows
Are emptied and lay a mess.

Bless those little souls
Gone to the best.
In God sweet words:
'From Ashes to dust
You're laid to rest'.

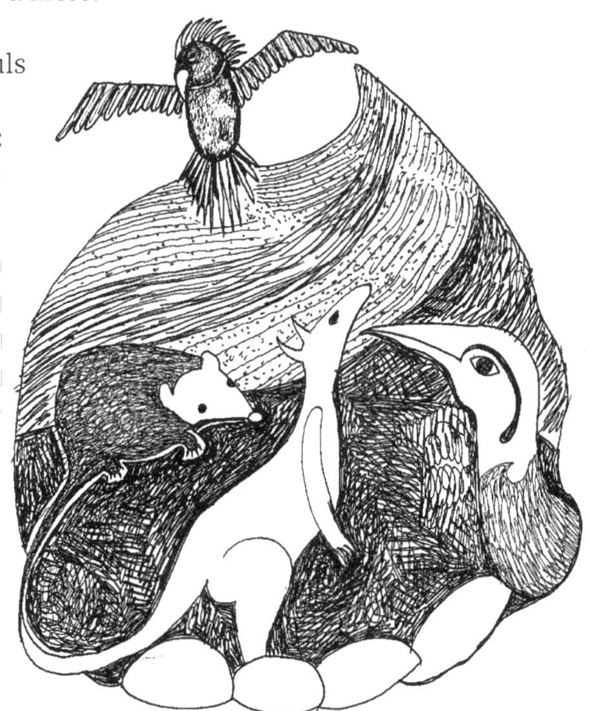

A BILLY AND TETLEY BLUE

I hear, I hid
I heed them swagman,
Sweep quietly out in to the West.
The towns people off Jennolan
Know when they're coming
And staying ... or sleeping
The night I guess.

Across them flats
It barely takes a breath
From marauding swagman song.
Them's brew fine billy
A tetley bunch with swaggies
Packed upon they punch
And carry on.

Along for their night
Of masquerading delights
Guarantees you up for a song.
A drop of shandy
From your pantry
In there buoyant laugh
And jovial remark.
You catch them a little bit prong.

On them plains
They squalor when it rains
And up and down these old fellas.
They're up for a game
Of enlightenment shame
Of months without
A pretty dollar.

Said Ned Stevens: 'You ain't
Takin my money or a pretty penny'.
To know my hard earned dollar'!

Swaggie replies: 'I'll boil my own billy
And make him look silly
I ain't waging as a collar'

A fight breaks out
And all lights out.
Like two mallee bulls
With a tank of fuel.
Of two raging old fellas

But when the dust
And all but settles ...
They sit and stir
And enjoy a kettle.
(Aussie brew in its finest mettle)
And all for under a dollar.

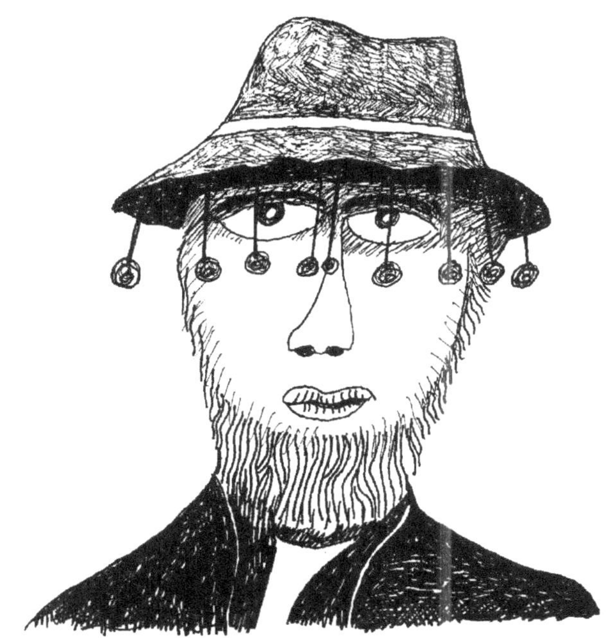

RICKETY RATTLER GHOST CARRIAGES (RED RATTLERS)

Rickety Rattler old train rusted.
Dusted nut and bolts jolted.
Together infused like old deer antlers.
Run-down inside with years of age,
And more broken bones
Then a soldiers grave.

Through hell and back In ghostly times
From the sixties to the nineties
And into the prime of its time.
Carry me back, slow to Western Sydney
Can't get to sleep,
With those piercing and screaming insanity.

As a young lad I heed the joy
Of riding red rattlers in times of ploy.
A little battler I'm one of thee
In old rusted carriages
Come ride with me.

Of rusted wheels made out of steel
Strong and tough as the man of steel.
But not fast and agile, like a bullet train
Made in Oz and powered by Sydney Rail.

Away from the bright lights
I adhere that's Sydney
Give her a coat of red and she's so pretty.
Jolty like an iron tank
To save me from death
She's a Sherman tank.

To the foot of the Blue Mountains
Its chugs along, I hear it tinker
My mind carefully 'til the last prong.
Many hours I hope for thee

Arrive but tainted she'll carry me.
As every minute, it passes the hour.
I will brave 'til the dying hour.

Ride I-kid-thee-not from the heart
Nor luxury you bring
Or flowers from the start.
Less terror and nightmares,
You delve saves me
From the spell
You cast upon me.

For the little Aussie battler
That prides himself.
I hope my kidney and heart
Breathes life for itself ...

Fire and brimstone it's a horror tide
I pray not to throw up
At the end of my ride.

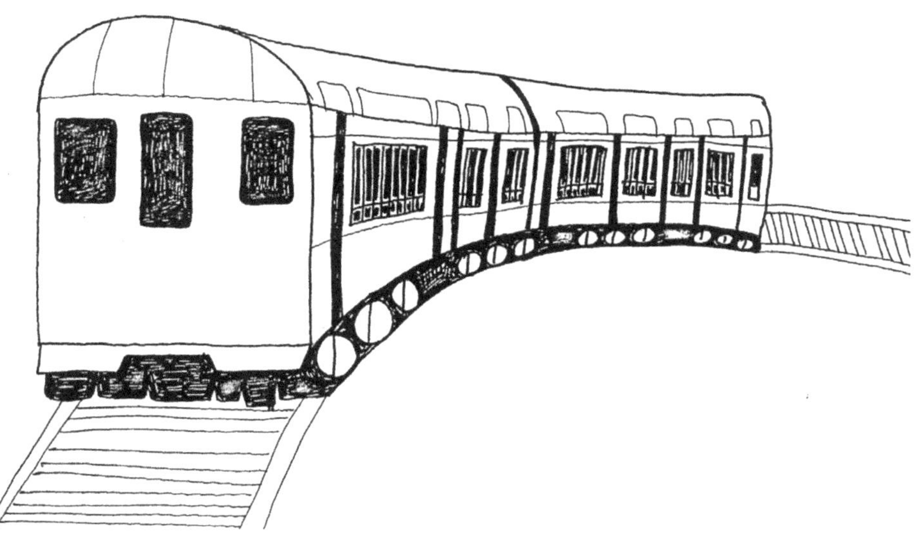

THE BLUE MOUNTAINS (THE BEAST WITHIN)

Come up, come up
For a breath of fresh air.
Come up to the Blue Mountains.

So lush, so lush with green trees
And rangers and ridges..
And plains as far as your eyes can see.

From streams and flowers
And Bell birds and Bowers.
And rainforests, brooks and springs.

A few explorers
Endeavoured to ignore.
Unless they walked
With indigenous trackers.

It welcomes you, it startles you
And hypnotises you on every occasion.
It's paradise with its native wildlife
It leaves you breathless
And captivated.

It starts out long
Entwines and turns,
And meanders and bends.
And turns into a great big serpent
That eats from the palm of your hands.

It can be peaceful
Calm and selective.
And pristine with charm,
To royalty and devotion.

But then it turns into
A prehistoric beast,
And strikes and devours with intention.

So don't be fooled
Mother nature can be cruel
When your love is for ...
The temptation.

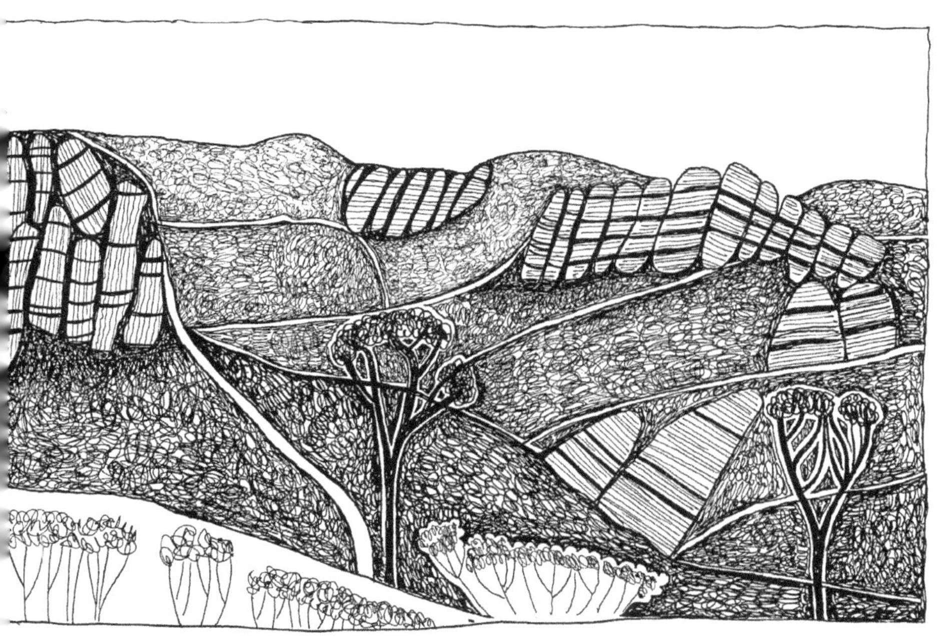

BOTTLE BRUSH TREE

Bottle brush, bottle brush.
Rainbow Lorikeets little crush
A noisy Miners little blush.

A sweet flavour for the day
And night time slumber for all nay.
And for some furry friends and some grey.

Sleepy eyes on a little stick
Nailed and garnished
And varnished and thick.
All in line and all entwined.

Yawning on a single twine
They race in slumber all in time
Green at first then turn to bricks
Soldered on strong with clever tricks.

Nor wind or thunder
Pour with rain.
Blows a gale
But never unchained.
No time to unwind
When the sun shines.
Coax you out
As the sun binds.

You shine and blossom
A fine flower.
Like a Christmas tree
Though months to dour.

Thou feels like a feather
But bits like leather.
Your sweet aromas
The sweetest nectar.

Crimson red
And Aussie flavour
A drug for those
Little feet who saviour.

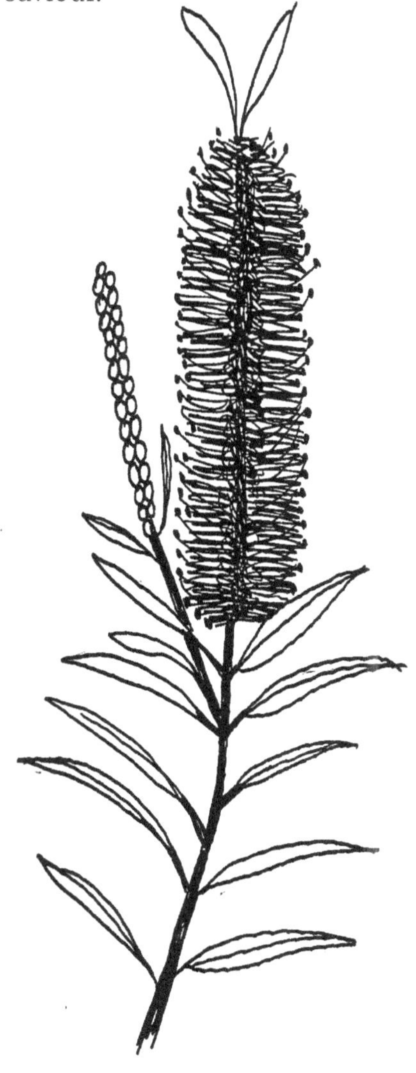

THE '1982 KANGAROOS' (THE INVINCIBLES)

Those rampaging '82' Kangaroos.
Ran riot throughout the UK
And Europe without a bruise.
Like a whirlwind tornado they came
In the form of rugby league legends
From our game.

The greatest Kangaroos
Called the Invincibles
With 'Biscuits' and 'Thrower'
The Captain and Coach
Respecting each individual.

A legendary side
It speaks for itself.
Lets dust that old trophy
From that cabinet shelf.
A few old heads
And young from the past.
As we gave plenty of stick
To the old dart.

'Albert' laying the foundation as prop
The old 'Rocket' intimidating
And as wily as a fox.
The old 'Pricey' gangling about ...
And a young argy bargy
'Les Boyd' taking heads off
Without a doubt.

A young raging bull
Called 'Jnr' (Pearce) locking horns.
And a mix of old and youth
Out in the backline
You know them of course.

We had the prince of five-eight
'Bert' swerving and setting up tries
'Sterlo' dodging and jinxing
Those pommies out wide.
The old 'Sludge' rolling in the mud.
And a rampaging young giant
'Meninga' fending them off.
(What a centre combo).

We had the greatest 'Guru'
(Was all one way traffic on one wing)
And fast 'Bowie (Boustead) on the other.
And a Wagga boy called 'Brentnal'
Who could fly like a bird in the sky.

We gave it to dads army
In the first test, and second of course.
And by the third it was a white wash
With 'Moose Mossip' having a dig
At those old Pommies of course.

The '82' Invincible's
We'll always treasure In our heart.
As memories of a young 14 year old
With Rugby League in his heart.

THE LEGEND FISHER'S GHOST

The 'Ghost'
Of one less likely,
Fred Fisher was never short
Of a penny.

Diabolical but a charmer
This old dart had a history
Of being fancy.
(As a convict
He was rather gantry).

Whose life was
But cut short.
By a less and likely
Old adversary.
Too make a small
Pretty penny
(He dabbled with those less unworthy).

He bided his time in gaol
For an unlikely little pardon
But his unscrupulous little coil ...
Was the scheming old George Worrall.

Legend
Has to be told
In 1826, of a cunning
And vicious foil.
To kill Fred Fisher
For his must love assets.

Upon his death
By the creek.
His ghost appeared
And pointed outward …
To a lone John Farley.

Whom stumbled into town
With fright.
As Fishers body
Was found in broad daylight
For George Worrall
Was later arrested.

And trialied and later hanged
For his ferocious crime.
He played all his cards right …
Except for a sultry hand …
He would later regret.

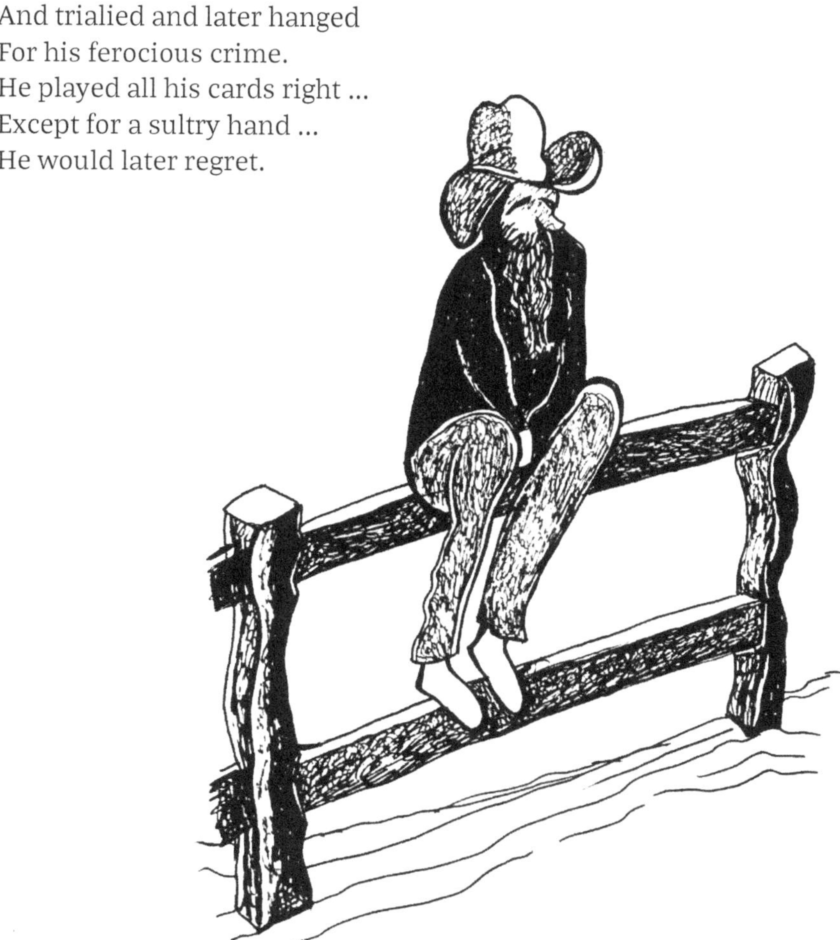

TASMANIA (THE LAST GREAT WILDERNESS)

Misty mountains
Shadow and darkness.
Sun and water
Leering with blindness.

Propagate and humble
Preserved and binded
Wrapped in green terrain,
Succulent and glows
With richness.

Cold air rises.
Echoes of nature.
Prehistoric mountains.
Millions of years old
Spiritual soul.
Indigenous.

Subdued and vast
Wild wilderness.
Covered in frosty terrain
Ghostly icon
Footprints embedded
In ice and stone age capsule.

Ever wondering plateau
Quite and lone silhouette
Full moon rises.
Giants propagate
Clusters of forrest Everglade.

Valley and rivers united.
The earth to ever
Reaching stars.
Tapestry embroidered
The air custodian.
Seep undulating
Communication.

And lush and green
Velvet blanket.
A rainforest of
Spiritual oasis.

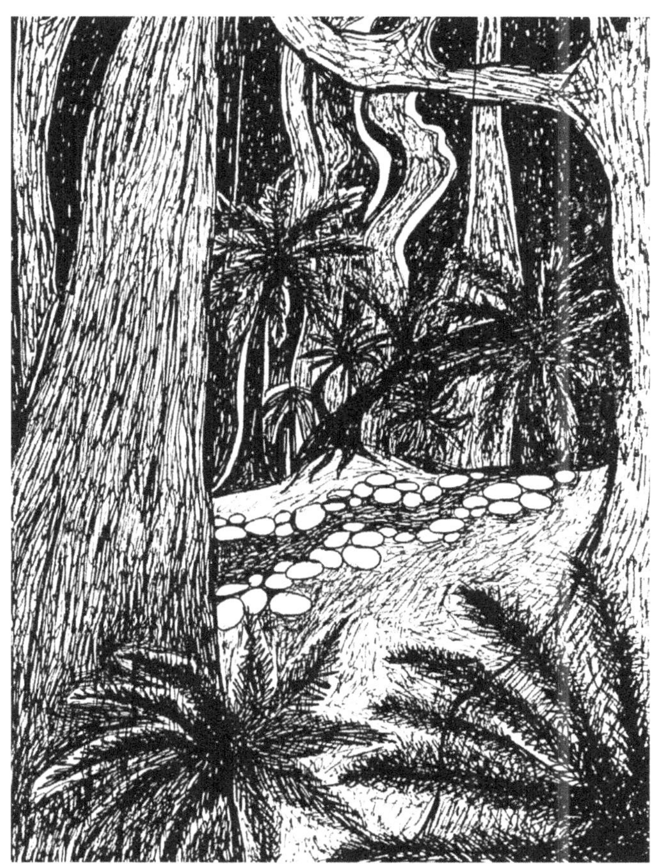

JIMI HENDRIX
(CLUB 27)

Star spangled banner
Your soul bestowed upon her.

UK was your adopted land
Welcome to electric lady-land

Rock guitar whizz.
All the glamour and rockstar glitz.

Ahead of his time.
A true genius and times sublime.

A time oblique
But extraordinary
And quite unique.

The 3 piece 'the experience'
A band of gypsies of little relevance.

Psychedelia, the word for peace
1960's all that purple mist.

A mind full of love.
Humble flower child
Bestowed from heaven above.

Walk the narrow line.
Hallucination and pure divine.
A love forever entwined.

The guitar.
The holy grail.
Humble, never betrayal.
All of 27.
Live fast, die young
With decadent.

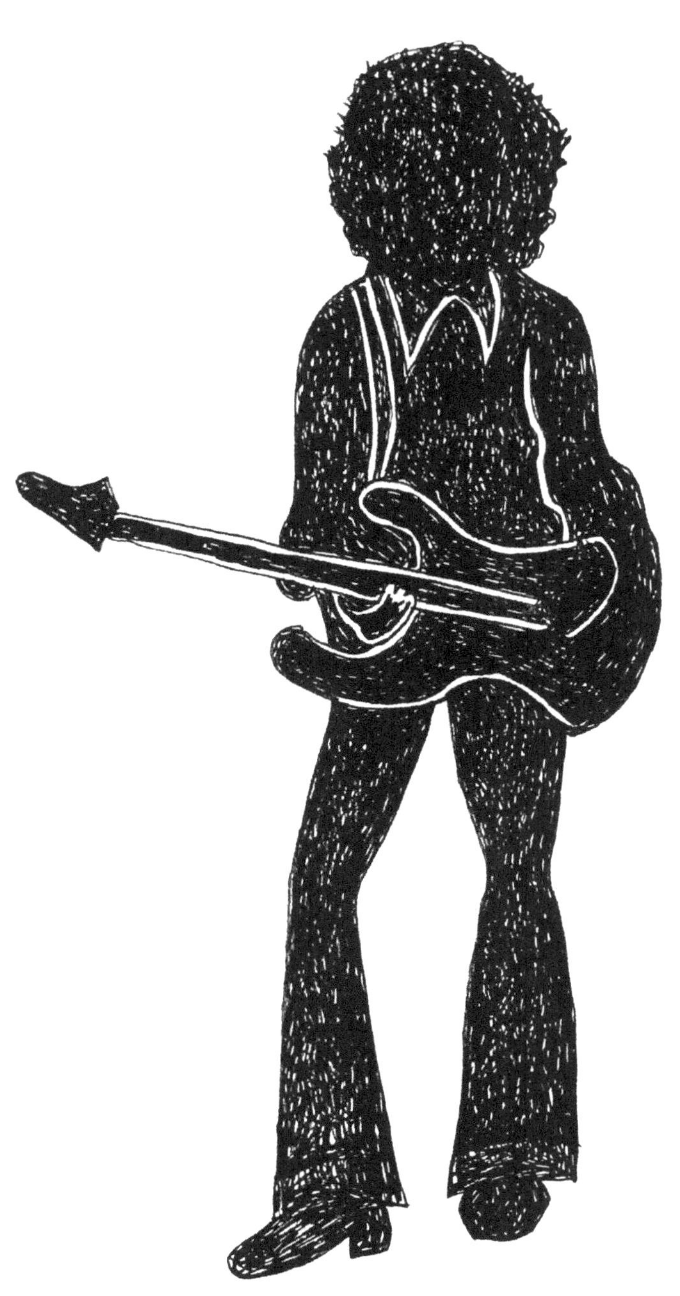

BUSHRANGER
(THE GALLOP)

He gallop, he gallop:
Over the mountain he goes.
Through brooks and stream
And seethe and snow ...
Into the great southern land.
Through bushland and eucalypts
And green fields, billabongs
And rivers that flow.

He gallop, he gallop:
Throughout this vast land
Into the wilderness
With his band of outlaws.
Searching for riches
And robbing the rich
On their land.
Even the mailman
For his paltry thruppence
And worthy shillings
In his hand.

They gallop, they gallop:
For the big money and gold
And high stakes it commands.
And a paltry bottle of rum.

They gallop, they gallop:
Into the town they ride.
Robbing and looting and drinking
And shooting
Almost till the dawn.

The gallop, the gallop:
Officers of the law
Constable write out a reward
For the head of the faithful four.
Through bushland
And native land
They chase the bush band ...

As they gallop they gallop:
The bushrangers take their stand.
And a shoot out with the police
As they drop to the ground
In both hands ...

The gallop the gallop ...

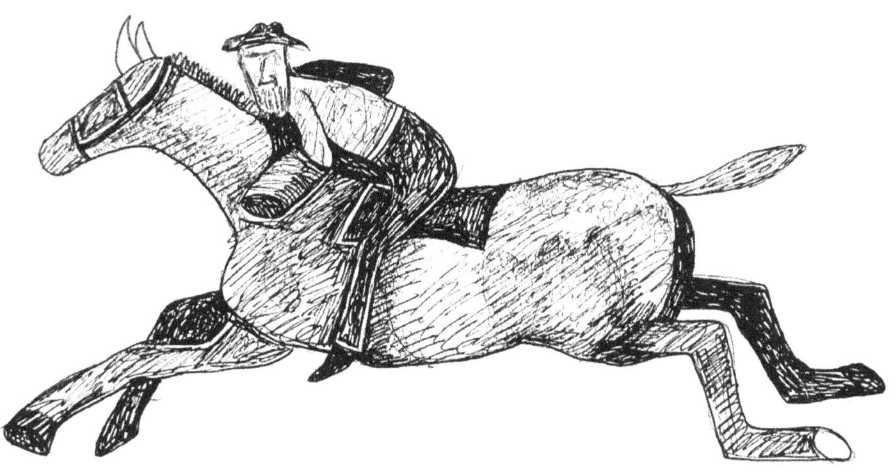

EUCALYPTUS TREE (OLD GUM TREE)

Oh old gum tree standing tall
Wilted and jilted
And weathered the storm.
Of centuries and time
Expand and bind
And tides and bides
With thick hide that shine.

Healthy leaves, to withstand the heat
From summer, winter
And bruises that leak.
Your tall and grandeur
Skyscraper in the sky.
Jilted and gilded
To rise above my eyes.

As far more splendour
As you stand alone.
With crisp cold air
You've nurtured a soul.
And coaxed the air
To be your cloak for a lair.

When bushfires heed
And calls no warning.
To collect the ashes
And bury the dead.

You seldom gaze
At the stars at night.
In the middle of its winters plight.
When I can smell the minty pine
And a dash of honey
To reap my mind
Its rewarding.

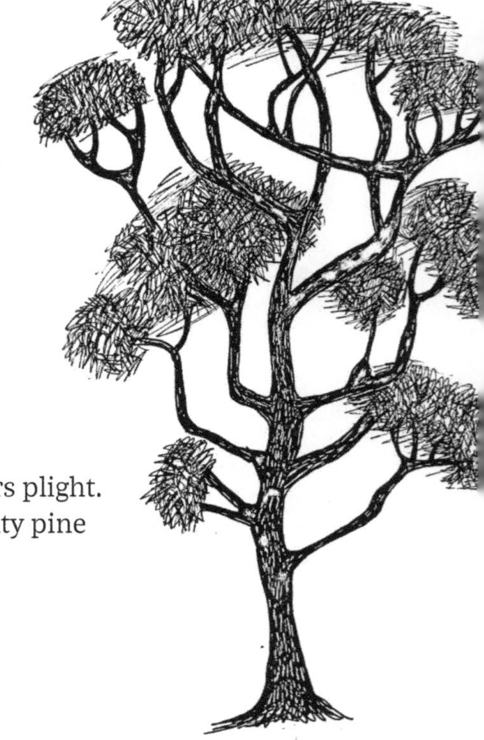

You stand upright
But unlike so many others.
That are small and contrary
Fall like brothers.

Your a home and comfort
For each and every little soul
Your nurtured and farewelled
From birds of a feather
As the Kookaburra and Rosella.
And Ants and Bees
And sleepy little Possums.
Tucked away in little cravats
And squeaky fruit Bats.
(That sway on your branches).
And even Bell birds
That tend to your flowers.

You roots grow old to find solace
In billabongs and your stump
Buried deep in layers of ashes.
You must be hundred of years old ...
I'm guessing that.

CONNOISSEUR

I walk that fine line
For a dime and dandy.
I work my time
For a much needed shandy.
And I eat my food and wine
As if it's treasure.
It's those few things in mind
I'm a king to my tither.

With a taste in mind
And the purist of divine.
It's flavoursome of a kind.
I have that inkling of an eye
Even if it's for a dogs eye.

If it drips and draps and spins,
Steams, fry drys your eyes
Or makes you cry.
Boils and coils and spreads
And bakes, pops, molly coddles.
Bake, roast and toast.
Or how to devour, eloquent dining
To traditional hand-me-downs to the latest
of fancies..

As eating at a bar or in a simple little jar.
Or to atone in a fancy 5 star restaurant.
To adding a spritzer to your glitter
As succulent and fresh
As saltwater crabs.

Waited on, as a guest.
Crystal and silver
And white trim tables
Elegantly pressed.

I sip a glass of a big bold red
Absorbing my pallet as it goes to my head.
A smell and flavour with the purest of
senses.

I look at many food I deter and haste
Though a lot to be desired
As a lot goes to waste.

But the simplest I guess ...
It's not complicated by stress.
It's easy on the eye
And the taste of desire
And the flavour
To devour
But to die for.

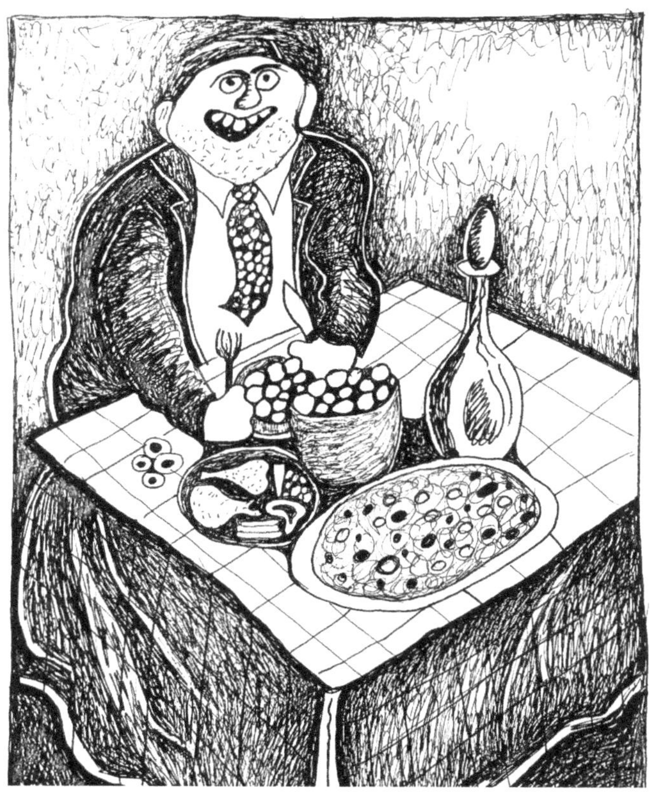

WAYNE 'JNR' PEARCE

Black and gold
Your story is told.
The local hero
Wore the green and gold.

A working class,
A gentleman with charm.
A legend, and the proud
Balmain Tiger.

Captain courageous
Played with vigour.
His heart on his sleeve
He bled through the riggers.
And with passion lay a very big ticker.

With eyes of fire, the strength of a bull
And fitness mentally to lead his pride
And beloved Balmain Tigers.

From that proud boy
That stood on that hill.
With legend's of old.
And a boxing old soul.

Through the wars of dust
And a muddy old yard
And in that proud old ...
Leichhardt oval we trust.

He made that number 8', heavens above.
Passion and spirit from a blue to a Kangaroo.
But never shed a tear, nor cry in defeat
Its how they breed them
Down in Darling street.

Played the game
Tough and courageous.
But to have it lost
In the grand final of ages.

In '88 and 89'
A mighty feat..
Wayne 'Jnr' Pearce.

A champion of ages.

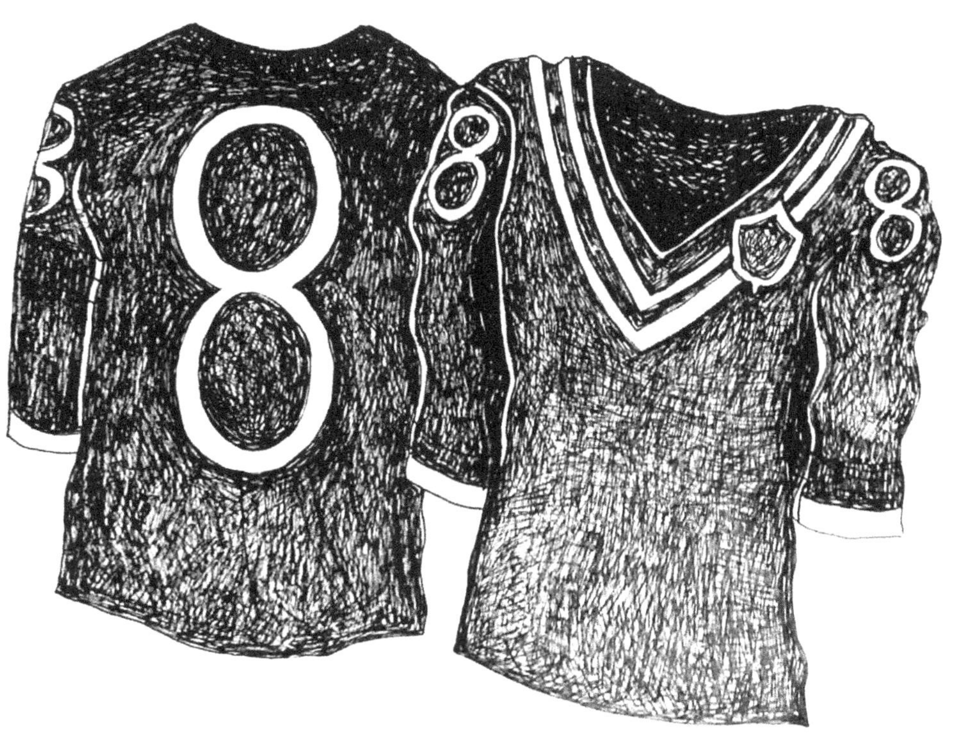

STATE OF ORIGIN (NRL)

Well here we go again.
Its State of Origin my friend.
Gather all family and friends
Around the fire again.

To those south of the border.
To the maroons far up north.
For barbeques and cold beers
To fire up a mighty thirst.

Those manicured lawns like a lady's nail,
The smell of cut grass enough to make you wail.
That time of the year when the proverbials appear
Everyone's a critic from the PM to the cynics..
As mums and dads and kids and their mates
To those roaches and toads fighting to save fate.

Teams guessing who'll
Pull on their boots first
And kick the losers bums
On that green turf.
There's pride and passion
To whom beats their Chest first
Or cry foul play
It's what Queenslanders do best.

There's war in the trenches
And in the dressing room.
As they pull on their jerseys
To become super human mules.

The maroon and blues
There's Freddie's chosen few
And Greenies babes maroon true and true.
Whether there shabby or bit subdue ...
As I'm true blue.

Its a kick and a pass
As beating a drum
Whether your drinking a Four X
Or a New or a Caribbean Rum.

Just make sure you leave
Your empties in the bin
As all the fans will be drunk rotten
By a quarter to ten.
There's more black eyes
Then a boxing ring.
It's called State of Origin,
It's in my blood it's in my genes.

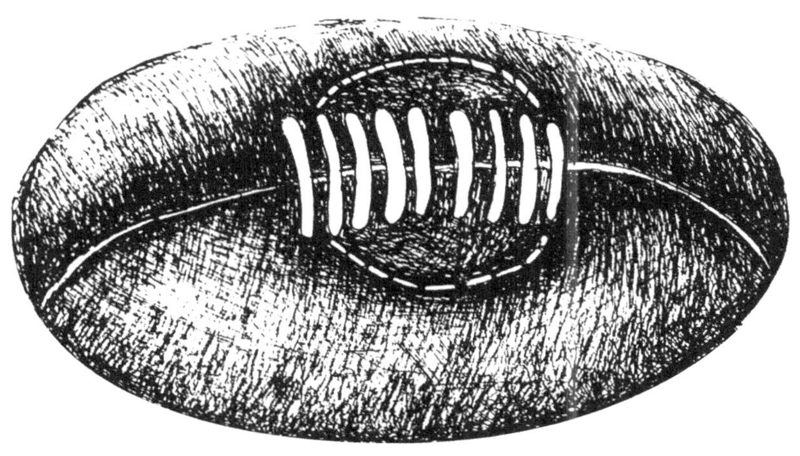

HALLOWEEN (FRIGHTFULLY SCARY)

Hello hallowed Halloween.
Its trick or treating time again.
Frightfully scary with a scream
Of ghost and goblins, ghouls and things.
No ones safe except
Young children with a grin.

Vampires and werewolf
And scull and bones ...
And headless torsos
Running after their own souls.
Over hills on hallowed soil
But not nor near no cobblestone.

It's a feast of gore for little teens.
No more surprising cos its Halloween.
Scaring and infesting little dreams
Of nightmares and shameful little schemes.
Mums and dads littered with kids
Out there trolling and looking for sweets.

Trick or treat is the worldly given
Sends a chill that's spine tinglin.
Houses are coaxed
And coated with glim.
The scary and shallow
And hallowy grim.

Laughing about in their best little costumes
As witches and warlocks
Jousting in the lounge room.
Black cat and spiders and bats
In the full moon.
Above spiralled in their mischievous mood.
Torturing and profusing
And spine tingling amusing ...

Frighting and screaming
As families find it bemusing..
As for tired little eyes we say good night
And big little good bye to say 'sleep tight'
A hallowed day we say goodbye
And for little monsters
Sweet kisses from mum and dad.
Owoooo!!!!

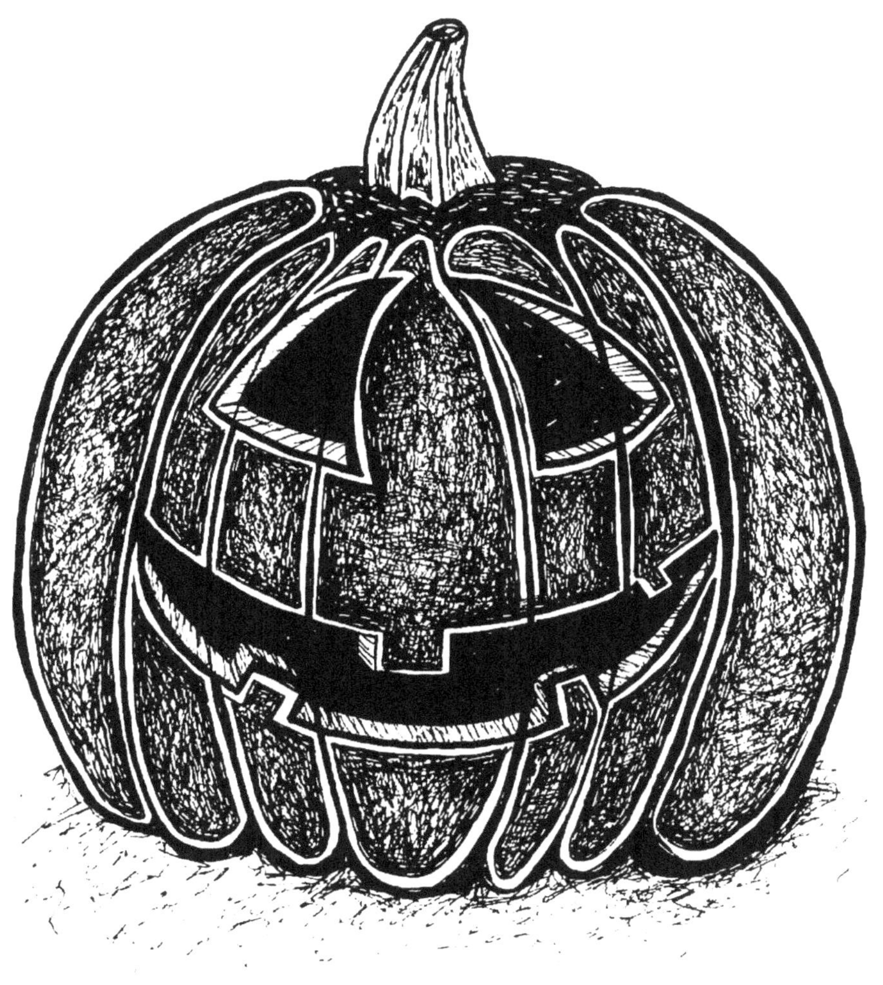

SHAMAN

Long my fore-fathers walked on thee,

Through land and bare necessity.

Through spiritual form he walked forlorn,

The Shaman he was by dignity.

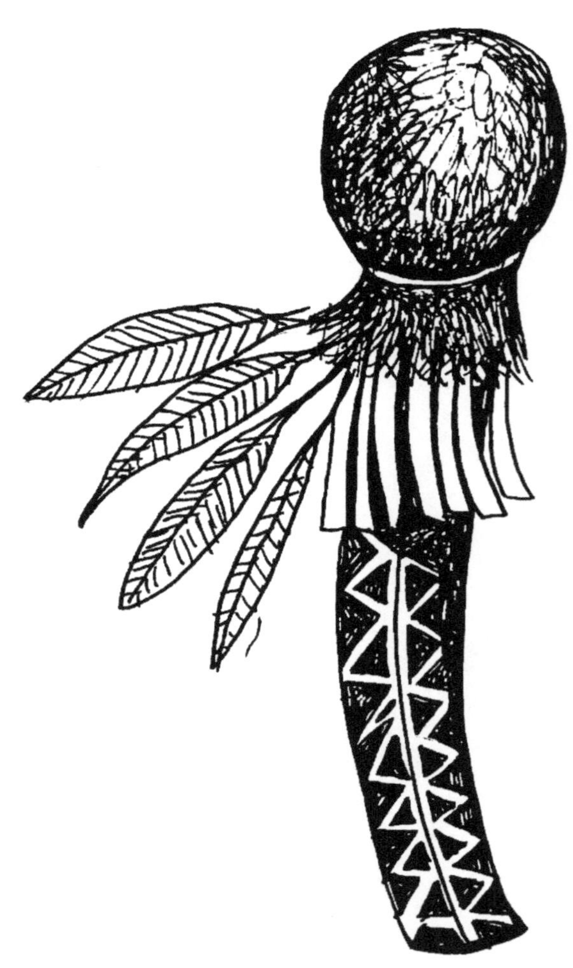

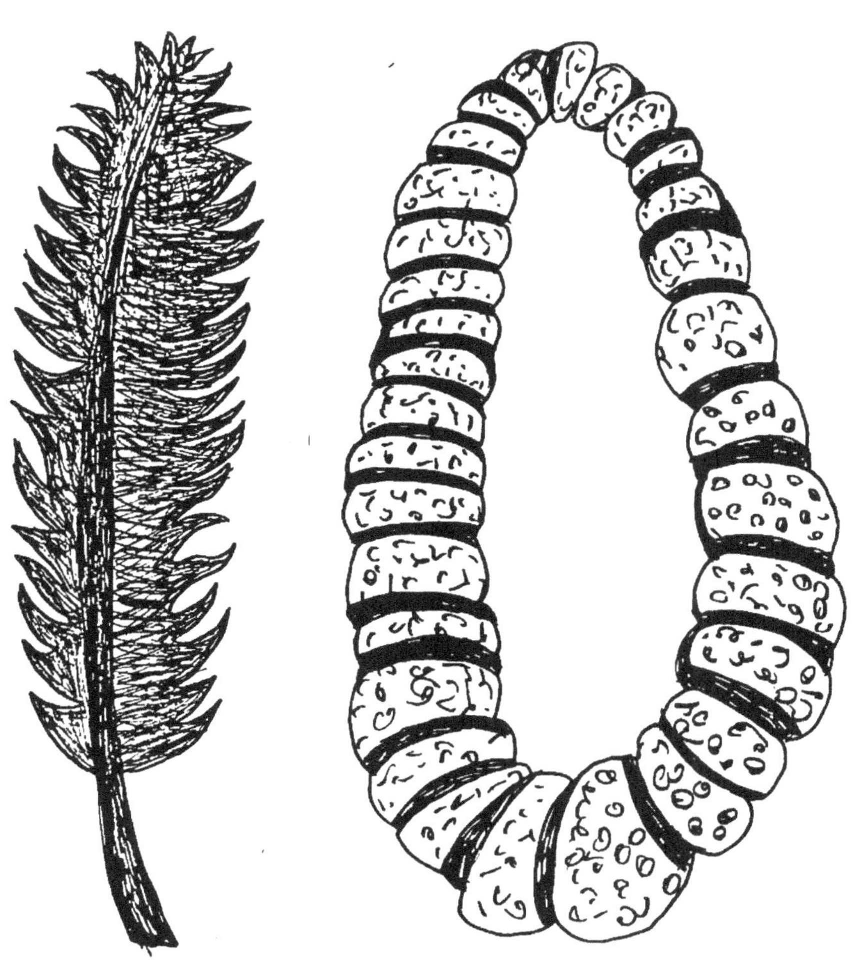

LEOPARD

Helter skelter
Spotted coat tenure
Camouflage, thicket
Solid bronze brisket.

Eyes of deep dark and mystique.
Pierced and reflective
Bone marrow subjective
Fangs blooded selective.

Eyes that shine, full moon bind
Wild with malice
Claws of talice
Savage and careless.
Gentle and defined
Pure refined.
Locked jaw and shredded
Carcass impedded unto trees embedded.

Sinister opaque
Lone, majestic
Solidarity and attentive
Predator. The Savannah
Stealth as you creep.

Canine, rip and tear
The hunter, the glare
The game to snare.

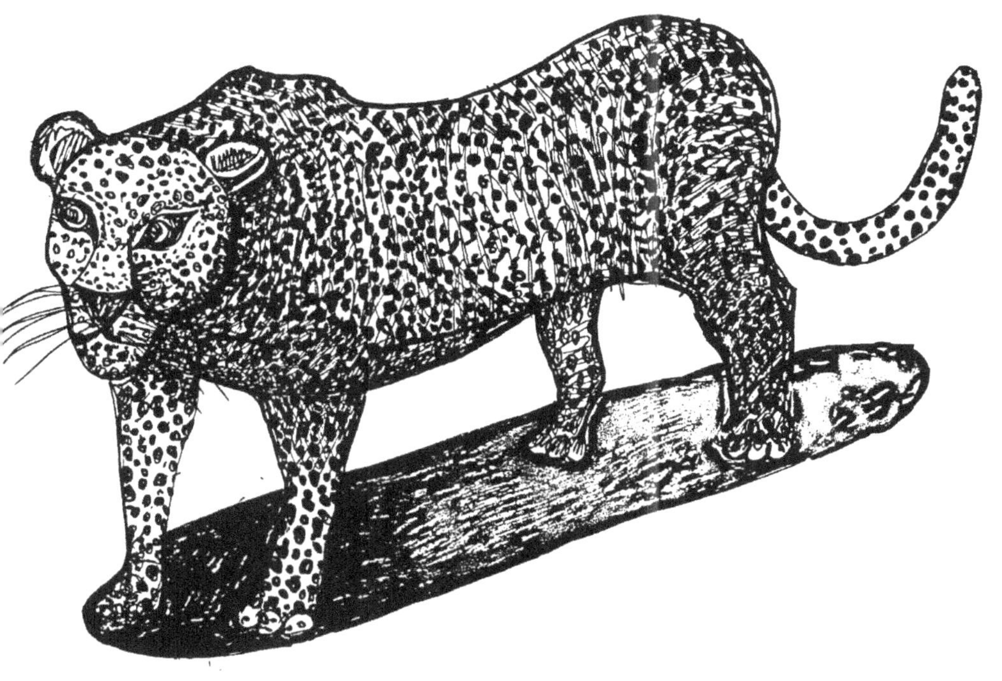

PENNY 'THE BEATLES' LANE

Wonder down
To Penny Lane
Where The Beatles
Stopped and refrained.

The working class
To earn a brass.
Sweat socks
And melancholy.
And to the upper
Class and folly

They harbour
Jovial smiles
With a hint of dry
And witty snarls.
As the barber and the banker
Squander up a ladder
And in their daily little banter.

The fireman rings the bell
In the aftermath of a sun shower.
As the sprinkling notes a dour
Enough to make the people sour

As people set up stalls
Of caskets for the poor
And to those enthralled
Live in closed windows and doors.
And baskets to steal a glimpse
Of what to squander right next door.

In Penny Lane
a heart is always refrain.
In London nearby
You see the pictures
Of the queen as her heart grows fond
Of her heavenly nature
As she gleams ...
Need we say more.
In Penny Lane.

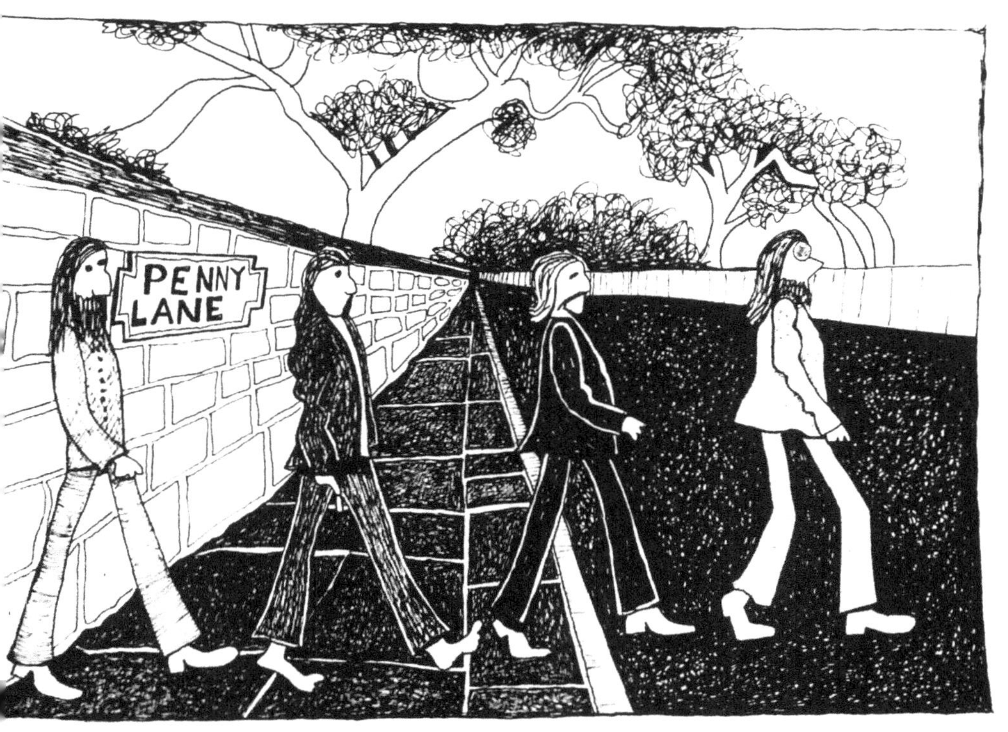

HOW TO MAKE A WINTER'S FLU

In one large pot
Either silver or grey.

With a large sealed lid
To keep little fingers at bay.

Add 3 cups:
Of winter month.

Enough to make you weak
And your throat so chesty
That you can't even speak.

A hint of winter breeze.
Just enough to make you sneeze,
A splish splash of morning dew
Like filling your eye lids with glue.

A few cold mornings
To keep you tucked
Away in bed.

A litre of rain that makes
A runny nose look dread.

Thunder and lightening
To scare you under the bed.

And the cold cold wind
To keep you locked away inside.

You mix it all together
And stir it well.

And what you have together ...
Is a fine fine concoction
Of Winter's Flu

Aaa Choo !!!

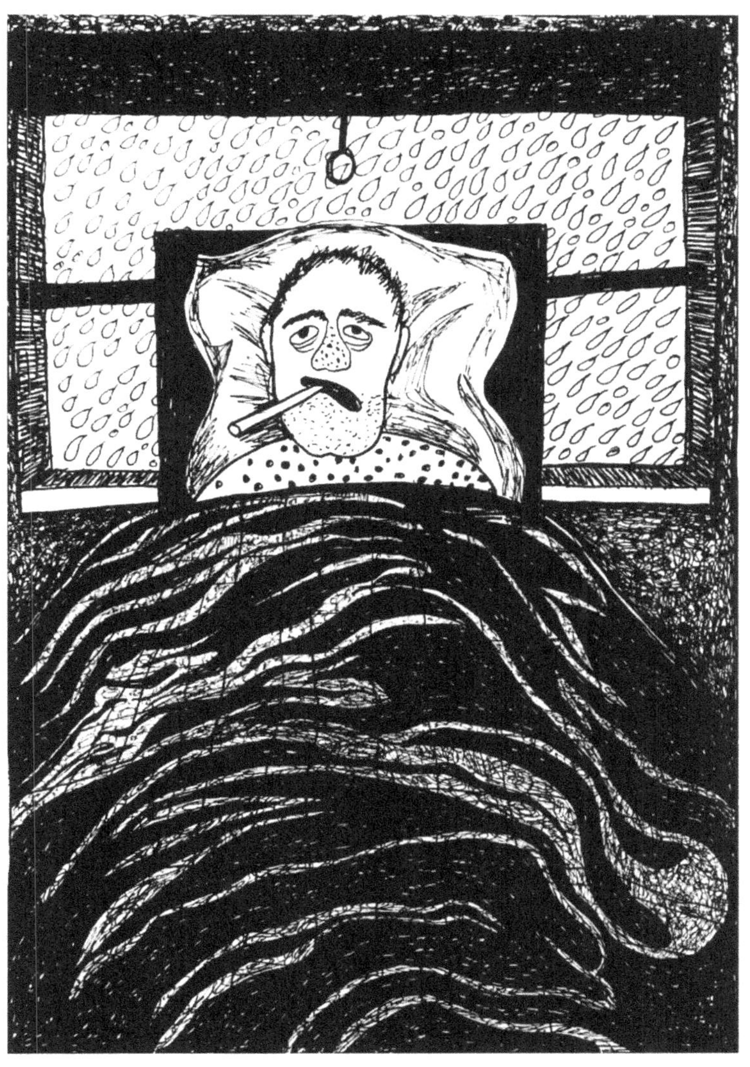

HENRY 'JACK' AVERY (THE KING OF PIRATES)

John Jack Avery.
A pirate he would be.
In 1694 this pirate roamed the sea.

Away from the motherland
To privateering for his own hands.

From the Atlantic to the Indian
Seeking fortune and treasures.

On the wuthering coastlines
Upon a compass measures..

A rusted merchant ship
He squandered and tallowed
As he lay low or be his head
Upon the gallow.

This pirate ship he mutinised
The Fancy 'twas free
A gallantry fast ship
With a crew of buckanee

To plunder all vessels
Be English or Spanish
He ascended into the Red Sea
For the Indian merchant challice.
(For all the gold and treasure
For what he could malice).

He wielded all his treasure
And off he went caboots
To this very day foward
His loot of precious jewels
Lay somewhere in cahoots.

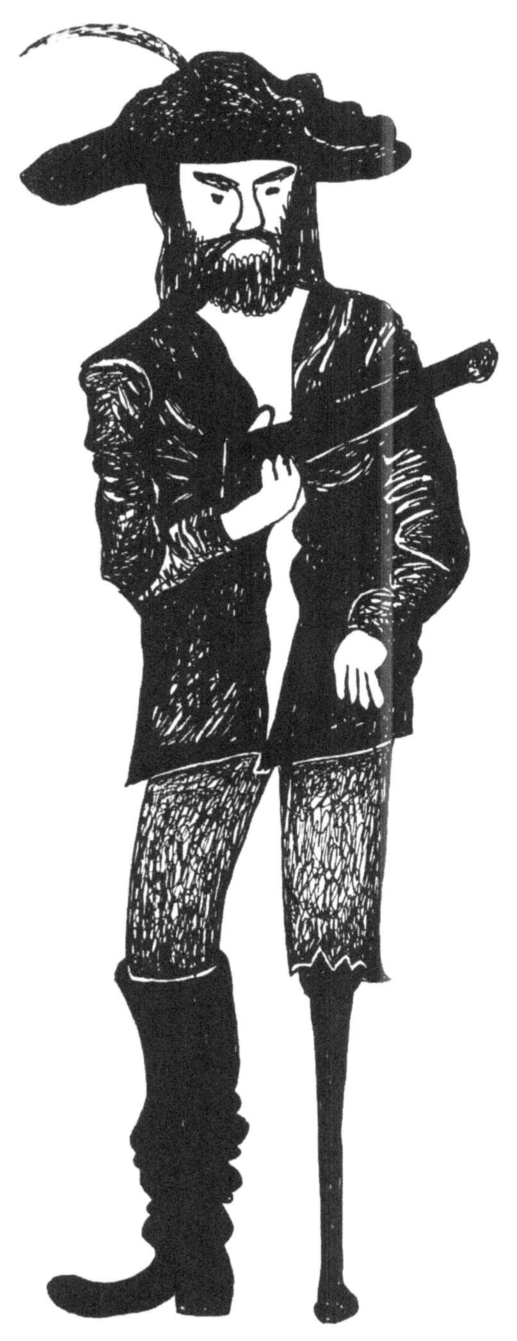

QUEEN OF HEARTS

Queen of Hearts
Queen of temptation
Of heroine and chaperone
And all them bad girl intensions.

Damsel be-jest, damsel in distress
Demure canteloupes go easy
On that little black dress ...

So cute and lovely
She could walk a mile so vaguely
She's no dowry to shake
That sexy arse so lovely

Lets talk the talk
And she can walk the walk
Till its time to come home.
She's a classy little chaperone.
Maybe after a few
She lays naked in perfume
In high heels and Corsica boots.

Erotic and exquisite
A lady of the news
Smile a can of cahoots
Or be in denial
And all that loving ...
To raise a smile.

Steals your heart abrasive
Erotic and vintage persuasive.
She's provocative, she'll break
Your heart and right from the start.

She's in a little town
Never far and I'm around.
Erotic intensions, my own intuition
With a strawberry bliss
She s little raspberry delish.

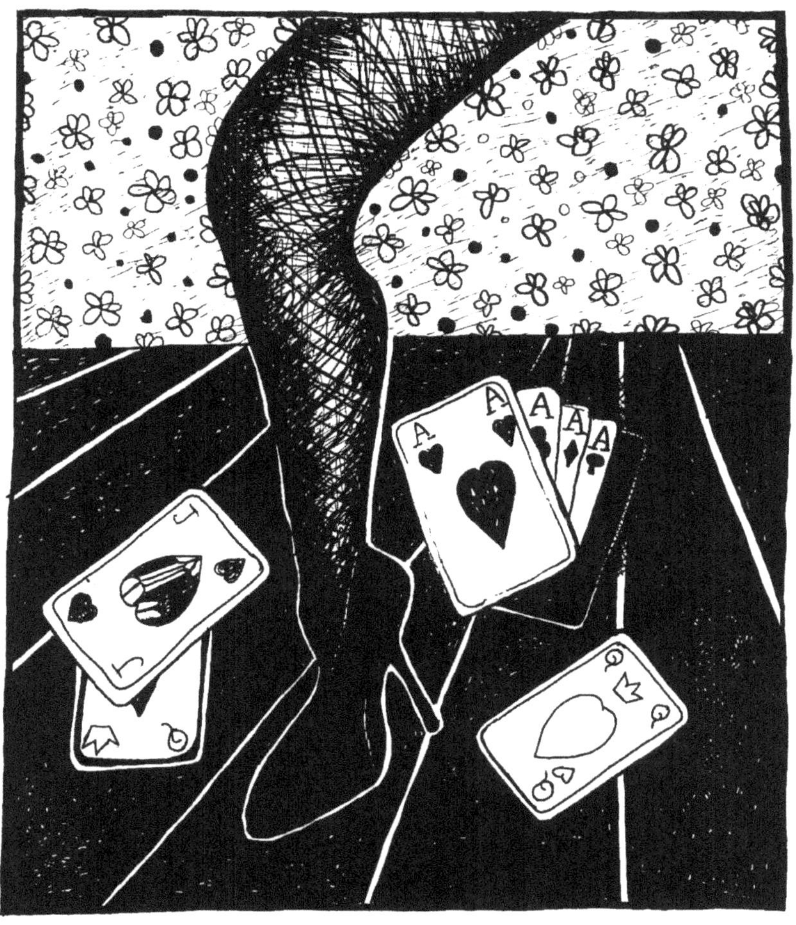

FROGS & TOADS

Frogs and Toads
Little eyes that glow

Shimmering glimmering
Croaking and ribbiting

Glitz and glammer
Little green tree lather

Tadpoles clinging
Eyes glistening

Musky odour
Rain and water

Green and gold
Dusky mould

Rubbery tuff
Smooth and rough

Wrinkles dimples
Pimples and rusk

Warts and spores
Slimy limey
Ooeee and gooey

A witches spell ohhh blimey not that
(Please no frog prince)
But maybe a cute little pet.

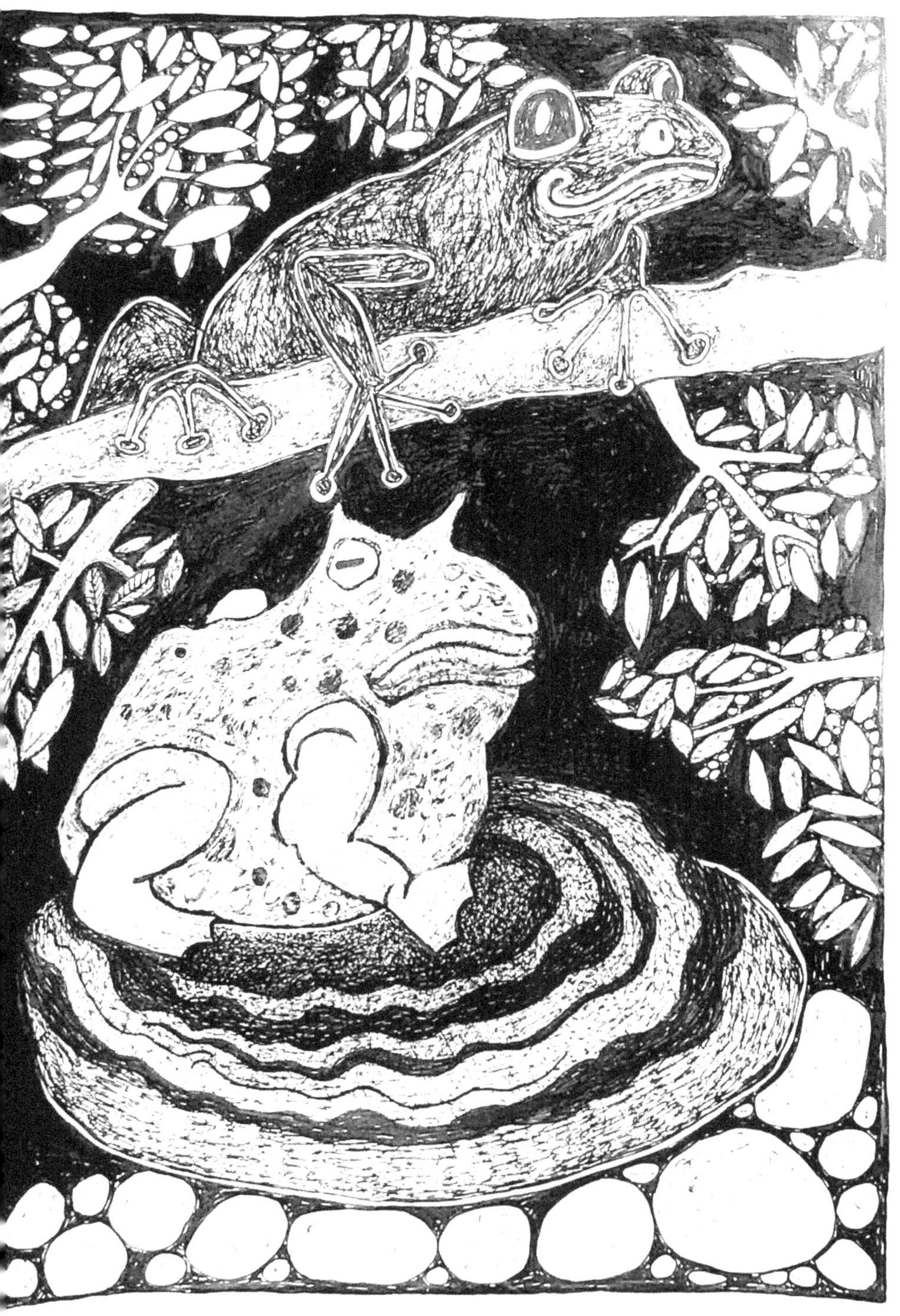

A WISH

Thy wish, thy wish
Hid in curtains of mist.

Though dour thy soul
How nimble thy bliss

Thou kiss, sordid
Thy fairest orbis
Mountains thou scalest
Amidst candles oblique
O thou darkness, abyss

Tranquil be thy fortune
On cowering notion.
Thou mind is penchant
Thy soul be merchant

Thou may succumb
To honorary jest
Thou conquer thy soul
Thy greed be thy quest.

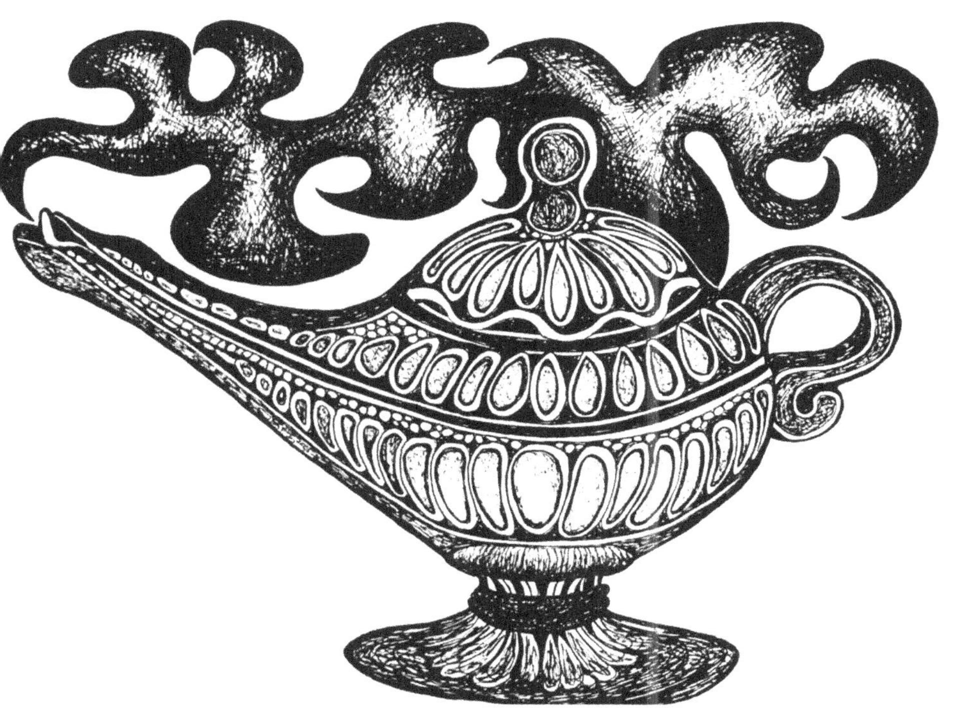

SANTA'S SLEIGH

Santa's Sleigh
Never dull or grey

With curves and twist
For pressies and gifts

In gold and iron
Built so divine

Red velvet and plush
With that added touch

For frumps and bumps
For Santa's cheeky rump

Built by hand
Elfish hand's

With added blush
Of elfish dust

Its shines so bright
As a starry night

Be it slow or steady
And fast and ready

Those reindeers galloping
As fast as lightning

Through heat and rain
Snow and the thickest of terrain
Even where water flows

Its never late
Always on time, at midnight
To deliver presents
For children on time

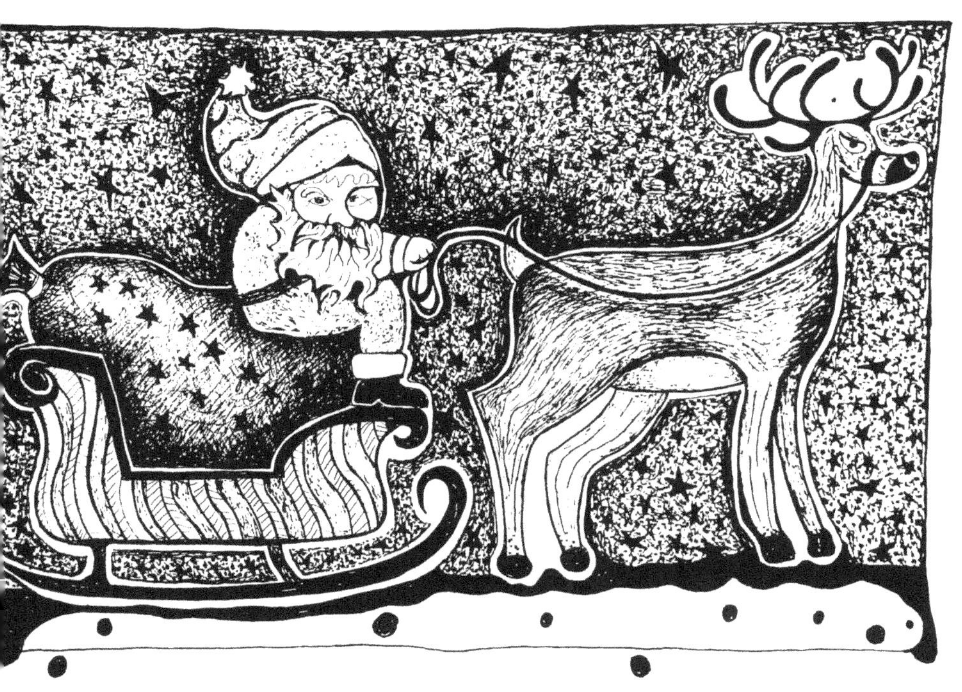

THE LIL' AUSSIE OCKER

The lil' Aussie Ocker
Or lil' Aussie battler.
Lives in all Australia.
Under one banner.

He's every lil' Anzac
As to every Sao biscuit.
Likes his meat pie
And Holden cars.
As cute as a koala
And acts like a galah.

He likes the hard yakka
And pays his bill.
Or cheering on his footy team
Just for the thrill.
A laze about type
All summer long.
Or throwing a sickie
Just to be a bum.

He's plain as Dazz
And smart as Kazz
Moody as Shazz
And likes to party like Bazz

He's a ridgy didge at
Times plays the didge
He wears his singlet
With his heart on his sleeve.
Stubbies and thongs
Or board shorts are a breeze.

He's fought in World Wars
To the Covid war.
Fought the bush fires
And the flood.
And the occasional pub brawl.

He likes to have a drink
Or shout the bar.
And luvs his bbq
And his Vegemite jar.
Loves his kids
And mum and dad.
His trusty dog
And his lil' wife Mazz.

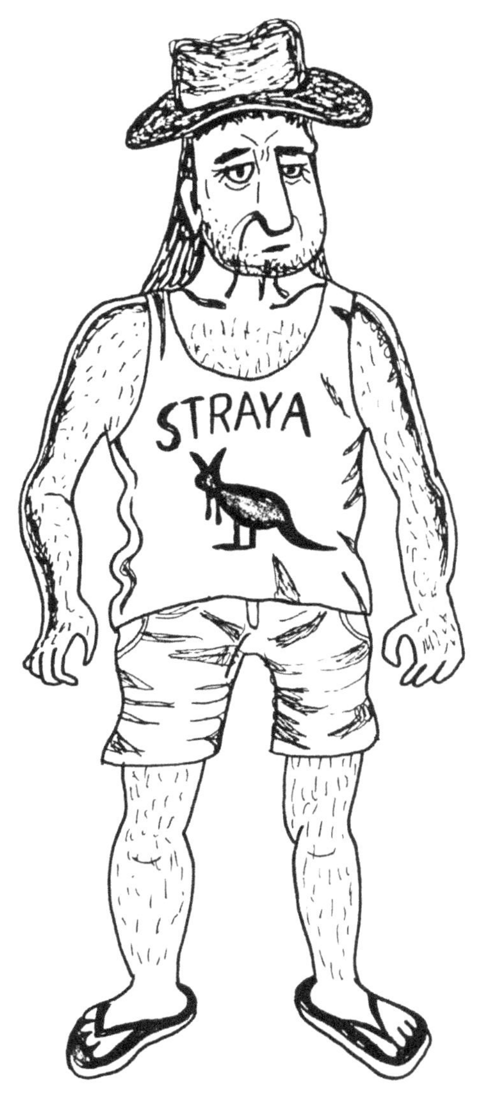

ROAD TO THE GOLDEN GUITAR (TAMWORTH)

With a crack
Of the whip
The muster had begun
For town's folk
And city folk.
And travellers alike.
The show had begun.

Buskers, jugglers
Bush poets and balladeers.
Boys and girls
And mums and dads.
Aunts and caravans
With their dog in one hand.

Through the blazing heat
And the dust and the grit.
Come one, come all
On the golden road.
To see the Golden Guitar
The glittering prize.
To see country music stars
In their finest hour.

A chance to meet Troy Cassar
Big Adam Harvey, Adam Brand
Felicity Urquhart and Sara Storer.
The McClymonts and the queen
Of country music - Casey Chambers.

And Lee Kernaghan and the ghost of Slim.
Sitting in the shade right next to Smokey Dawson.
And John Williamson digging his heels in
And having a spat.

So if your in Tamworth
At this time of the year.
Looking for a cowgirl
Or music for your ear.
Look no further
Than the Golden Guitar.
To kick up your heels
In the dust bowl jar.

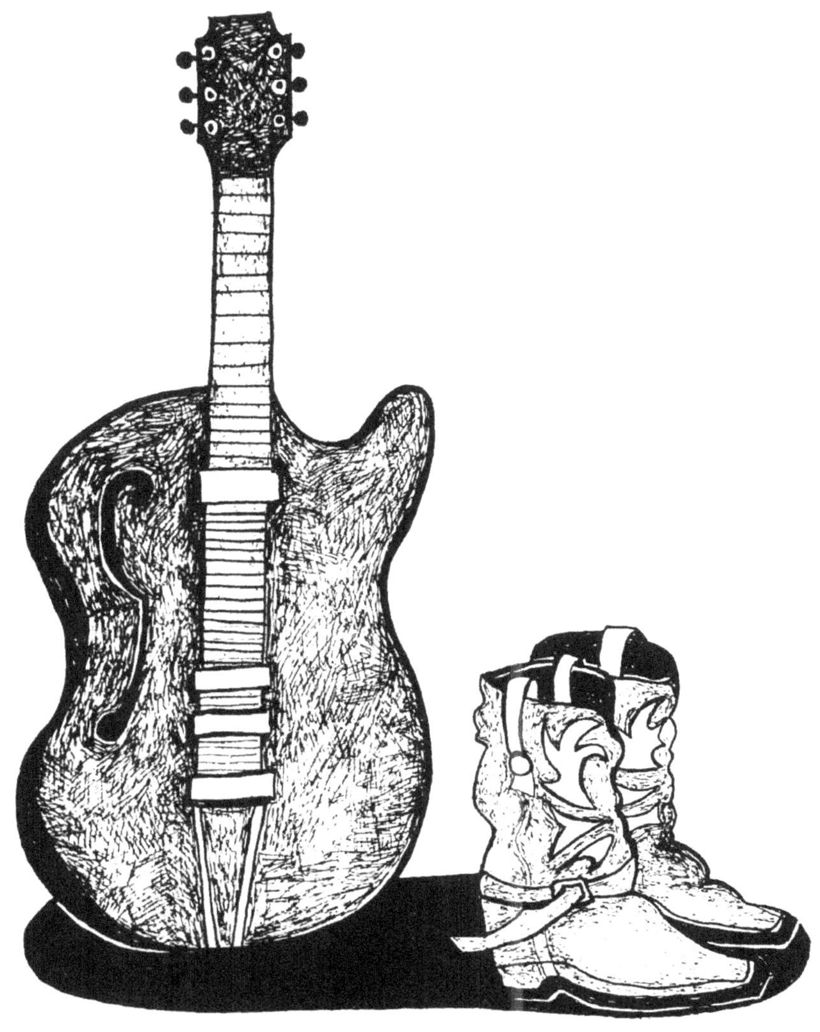

CHOCOLAT

Its dark, its rich and smooth
And creamy and irresistible
To your heart.

It awakens your senses
Like the morning sunrise
And all before midnight.

It's a kings treasure.
And Aztec gold.
Over thousands of years old.
It's worshipped and sacrificed
And conquered wars
From the age of dawn.

Its travelled abroad
On spice ships
And merchants
All over the world.
And fought over
For love and devotion
Be it irresistible in bed.

And loved by more women
Than men even children
It's a minor dread.
Its kept nice and tidy
And lays and sits
In its own little packet.

And folded into corners
To keep the aroma
And the flavour
In your corner store.

It melts in your mouth
As you savour the delight.
It's wrapped in silver or gold.
And it holds a place
In everyone's heart.
From such a humble beginning.

Mmmmm yummy chocolate.

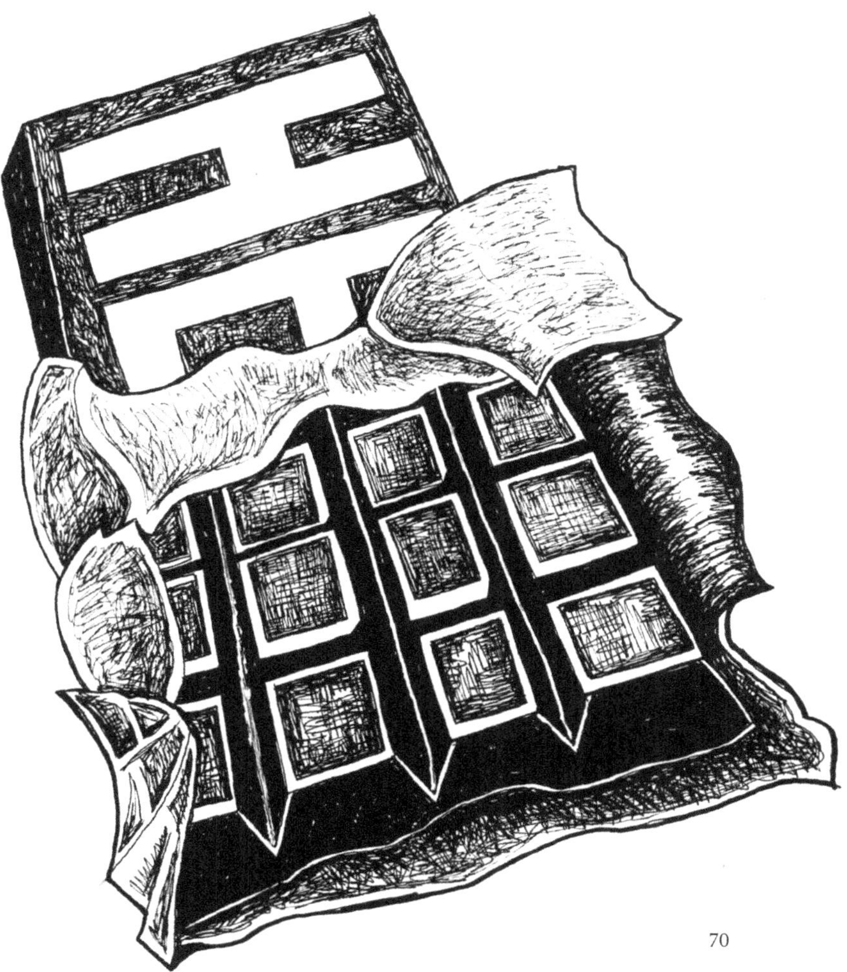

GOTHIC

Gothic your neurotic
And times very erotic.
Mind-full and insightful
Elegant but tranquil

Grey your quite a handful
But black you always graceful.
With darkness you shall remain
(A small but beautiful age).

Love and sentimental
Born and temperamental
Charming and resist-full
A curse of hallow grin
Stubborn within.

A castle you have built.
A rose in cast iron
Concrete and stained glass
Marble and glazed facade

Red wine and entwined
Lips full and sublime
Centuries defined
Darkness you posses
Night you're obsessed.

Ridiculed by zest
Famished amid fest
Mysterious and opaque
Bohemian refined
Rhapsody entwined.

All gothic and pure divine.

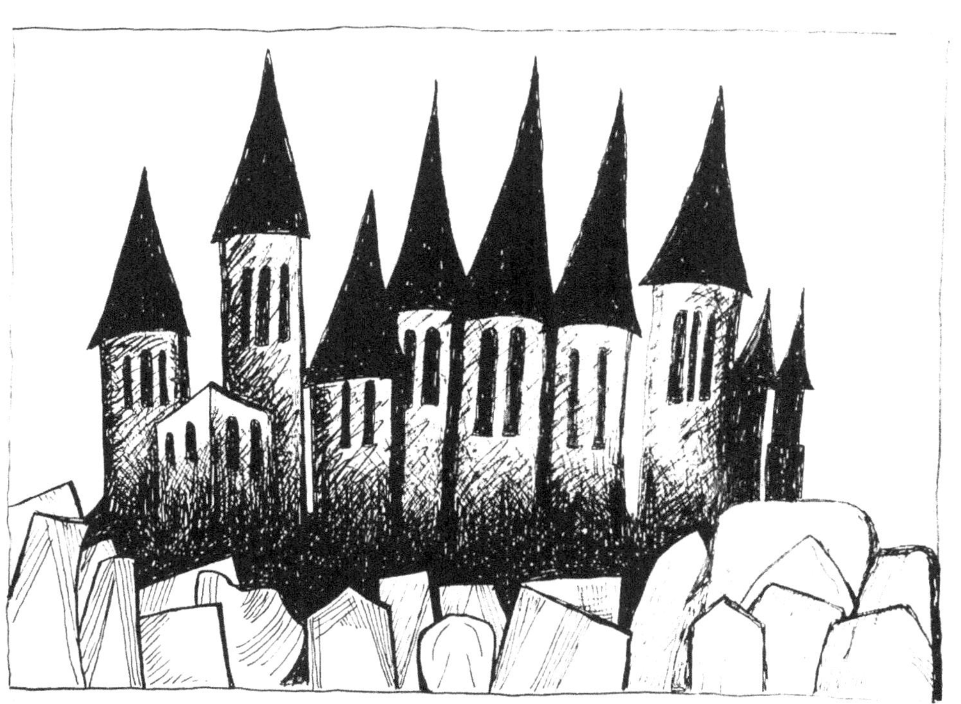

MY SUNBURNT COUNTRY (AUSTRALIA)

My sunburnt country
You play your game
So eloquently.
Whether your putting
Us through hell
Or being an angel in your shell.

Fire and brimstone
As you cast your spell.
Over hot and cold stone
Baking the Nullabor
And cracking the dry.
Or harrowing thunder storms
Way up the tropics the northern mire.

Heating and combusting
The outdoor air,
To the central tablelands
Your tainted full of flair.

Through bushland with charcoal and red earth dye
As painted in caves by the Indigenous fire.
To the billions of stars that light up the night sky.
Through cascading dams and over flowing dry land.
To the sizzling lonely desert on your kingship merit.

Cracking the furnace through undulating ash.
Down south cold winds of snow and thicken ice.
Through the rain and sea through spruce
And gum leaves.
To a temperamental rainbow to a roaring borealis.

Its baron, it's dry, its forest of dark, its burns of fire.
Its rich as it rains as it floods with terrain
Into the Murray and the Darling basin.

It breaks your heart and makes you cry
And it'll break your back...
'by struth I wouldn't have it
No other way of luck.

My beloved, my island and my home
I love and call Australia home.

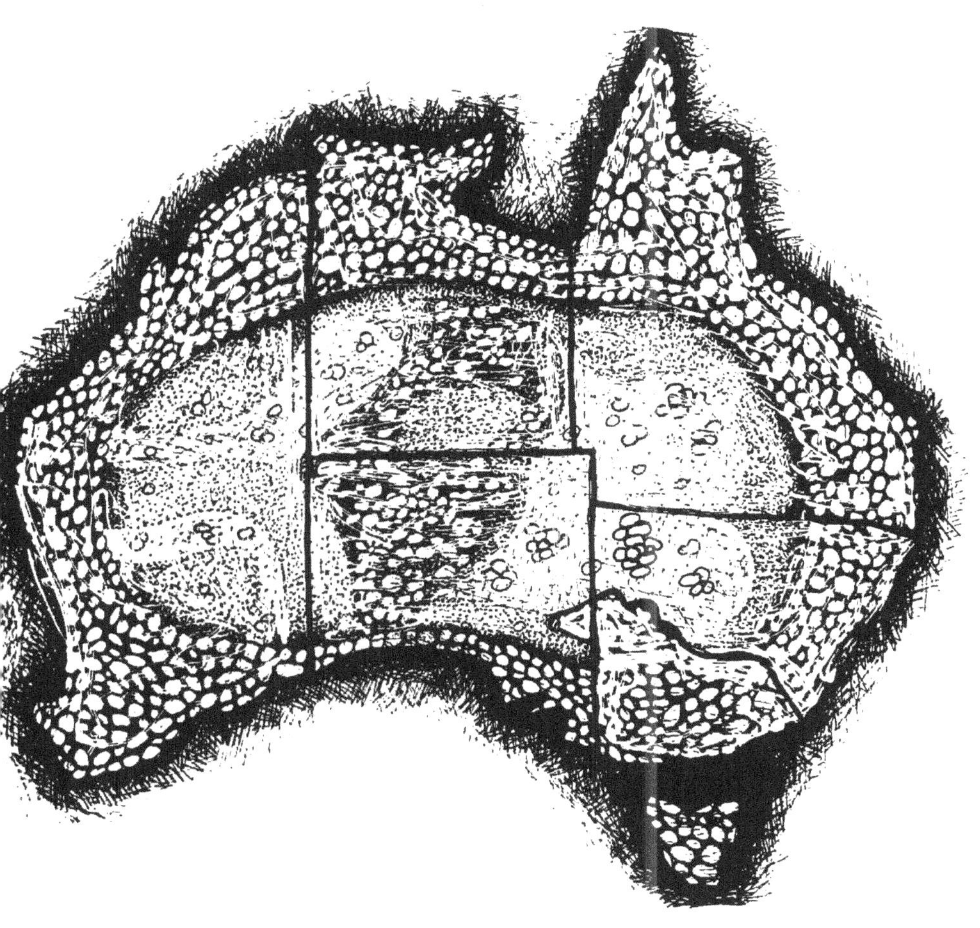

THE GOLDY MERMAID

Sophisticated lady
That lives on the coast.
She lives in a bubble
But not like most.

She weaves her magic
In balms and charms.
In pretty pink crochets
And brightly coloured yarns.

She lives for the sea
The playful type
Surrounded by her family
Especially a cute little tyke

Call her a mermaid
Or a siren of the sea.
She's damsel and old fashioned
That likes her afternoon tea
With strawberry scent and jasmine tea.

She's one of a kind
A little Aquarius in her own mind.
A mermaid from the land
To her ancestry clan.

She surrounds herself
In tropical delights
Much to the amusement
Of pleasantry types.

So if your on the Gold Coast
Amongst the aquatic delights.
Or basking in the sun
Or under a tropical palm.
She be swimming with the dolphins
During the day and night
Or sinking a summer shandy
Under the sombre moonlight.

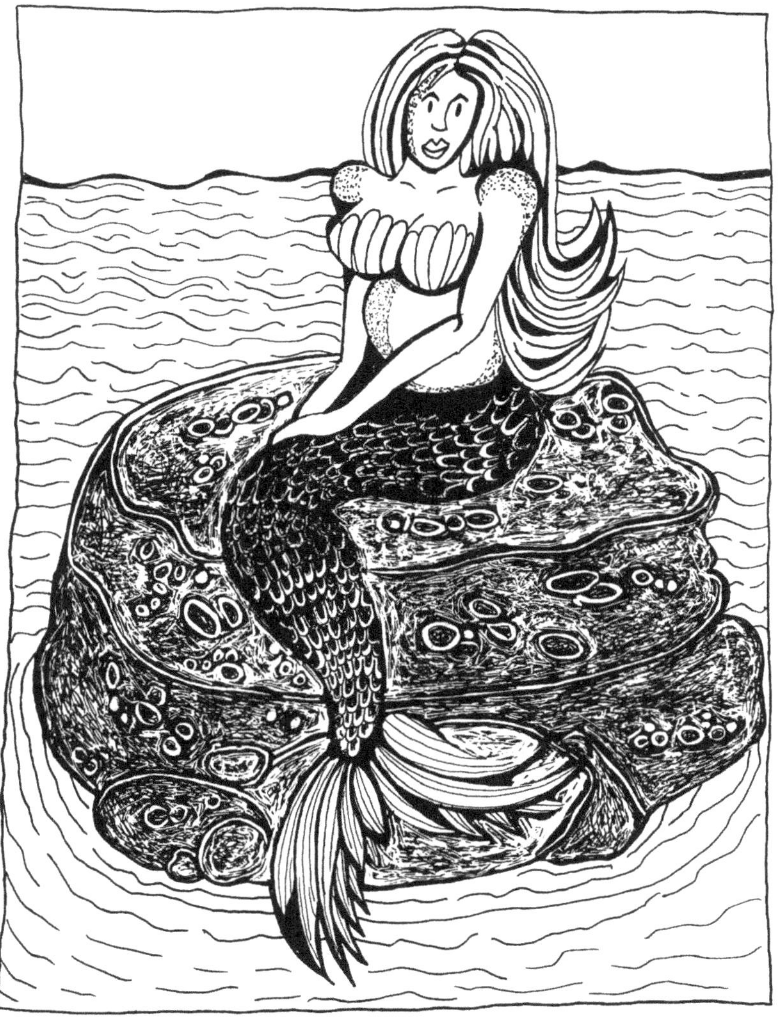

THE CURRAWONG
(DARK SHADOWS)

The Currawong glides
Through the trees.
Always busy and
Moving like the breeze.
Up and about before first light
And comes out with his flock
To give you a fright.

Sharp witted and
Sleek black all over.
And streak of white on his wings
And long tail feather.
Maybe a magpie with his little wit
But nasty and clever in every bit.

Black knitted and raiding
Through the day and early night.
Passing dead apples and lemon trees
As he snatches hatchlings
Like a thief in the night.

Before dawn stay indoors
Lock up your door.
As the air is sinister
With a cold and dark applause.

At times passing through
Black mulberry trees
With sheer delight.
Consummating and consuming
Like a black plague in full flight.

Flowing downstream
Like a ghostly shiver.
Eyes manoeuvring
And lurking about..
As he slithers into the cold breeze
Like a grim reaper.

Whistling and calling luring out.
To brave little souls tucked away
In their little cravats.
Every little soul adheres to stay indoors
In all the hours you just cant ignore
'Come out, come out' he lures and tethers.
And beckon and whethers.

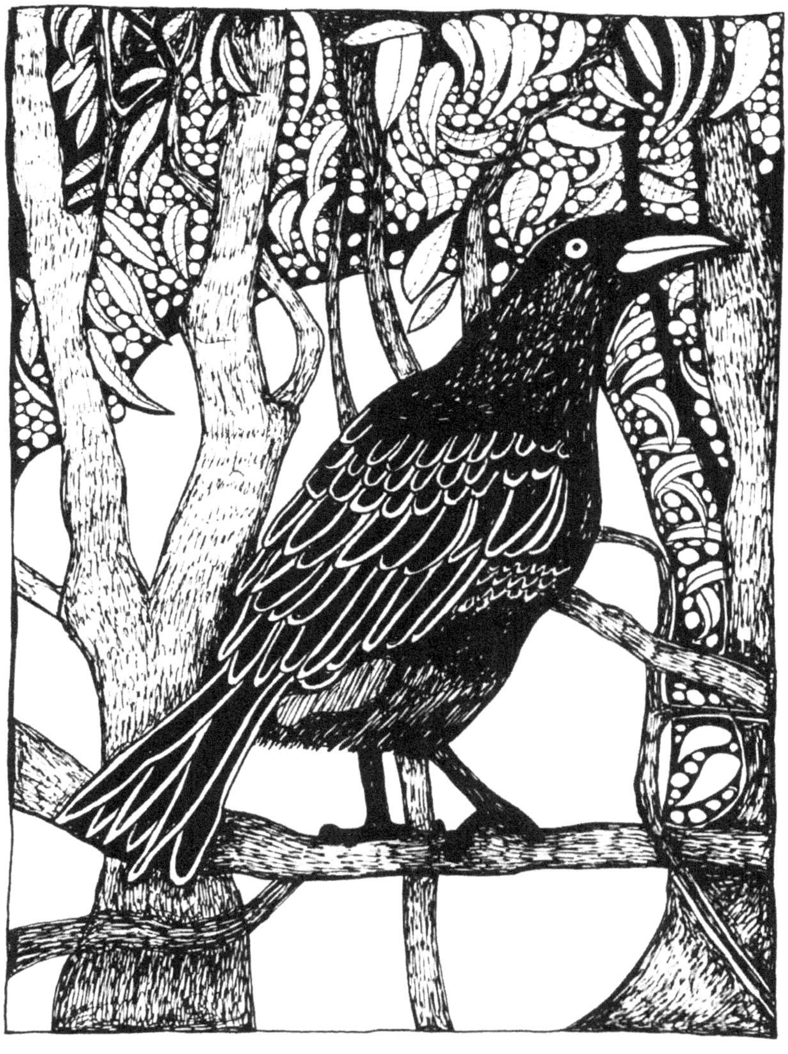

AUTUMN IN ORANGE (NSW)

Autumn in Orange seems uncanny.
As maples line the street so plenty.
Autumn shed their leaves so lovely
Scattering gold and yellow to blood red orange.
(It adds to that little bit fancy).

They line the street
The streets a little bit dandy.
Even the Aussie Eucct
Green and always envy.
A subdue little town
Full of calm, frown and down.
As miners and tradies
And fine wine and ladies.

Even shops will pause, with a lovely.
And show fine gold, jewellery and gentry.
Orange breathe's that country balm
Its face welcoming
It warms a country charm.
And times a bit ... you know narky.

She draws you within upon that hill
When its cold your feet
Can feel a winter chill.
From Mount Candobolis the ghost that rides
The train to Bathurst way late at night.
She's that chill that runs around town
In minutes it gives you a cold down frown.
You feel that rushing by in seconds
From the westerly's that fly in like a 747.

Over the mountains
Over the plains.
That Liverpool plain
Where it sometimes rain.

Then wait till its daylight
Where she picks up its pieces.
Then warms your heart
With her midday glitches.

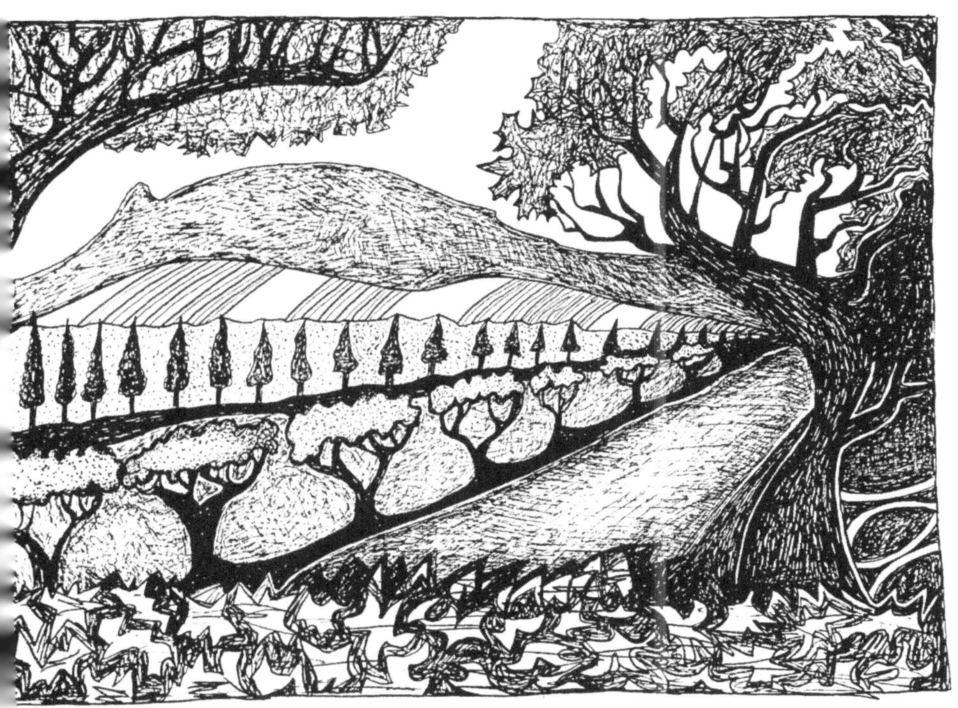